Are Kodavas (Coorgs) Hindus?

P.T. BOPANNA

ROLLING STONE PUBLICATIONS
BANGALORE

Are Kodavas (Coorgs) Hindus? – by **P.T. Bopanna** published by Rolling Stone Publications, Jayanagar, Bangalore – 560 011

◈ **C P.T. Bopanna**
144/1, Third Cross Byrasandra Road Jayanagar 1 Block East Bangalore – 560 011 ptbopanna@ yahoo.com

The author, P.T. Bopanna, takes legal responsibility for the entire content in the book, including the conclusions and opinions expressed by the contributors of articles in the book.

ISBN : 978-81-909765-9-6
Cover Design: Franz Mendonsa franz.mendonsa@gmail.com

First Edition : 2018

*forces of three Indian States.
He was best known for his contribution to integrating the police forces of the princely State of Hyderabad, into the forces of the Indian Union in 1948.*

Contents

AUTHOR'S NOTE

This book tries to answer the question 'Are Kodavas (Coorgs) Hindus?' I have involved some of the finest researchers from Kodagu (Coorg) who are knowledgeable in the matter, to find the answer to this pertinent question. To that end, this book is a seminal work on the religion of the Kodavas.

Being a journalist, I have tried to present the findings of both those who claim that Kodavas are Hindus, as well as those who maintain that Kodavas are not Hindus. The idea is to enable readers to draw their own conclusions, rather than thrust any particular line of thinking on them.

This is perhaps the first time since the world-renowned social anthropologist Prof M.N. Srinivas wrote his monumental work 'Religion and Society among the Coorgs of South India' (1952), that a serious effort has been made to analyze and debate the various facets of Kodava religion. Prof Srinivas's book is based on his ethnographical study of the Kodava community for his D.Phil degree at Oxford University.

I wish to summarize here the findings of the various writers who have contributed articles/papers for this book. My own understanding is that Kodavas are not Hindus. Though their original faith was unique and not in common with the core Hindu beliefs, the influence of Hinduism began with the Lingayat Rajas who ruled Kodagu for nearly two and a half centuries from 1600 AD.

The purpose of this book is to inform Kodavas, especially the younger generation, about their original faith and belief system. This may help them to better appreciate their original faith which is slowly being eroded due to the creeping in of Brahminical practices, as young Kodavas move away from their Kodagu roots to urban settings.

Dr. Chotteyandamada Sowmya Dechamma, an Associate Professor at the Centre for Comparative Literature, University of Hyderabad, who has done extensive research on Kodava language and culture, opines that Kodavas are not Hindus.

In her paper "Of Death, Rituals and Songs for the Dead: Kodavas and their Histories", Sowmya notes: "A cursory glance at the customs and rituals of most Kodava-speaking peoples show that they are neither idol worshippers nor do they include priestly Brahmins in any of their ceremonies. All their festivals revolve around agricultural practices and none in the name of any Hindu god."

Prof. Neravanda Veena Poonacha, who retired as Director of the Research Centre for Women's Studies (RCWS), SNDT Women's University, Mumbai, has been critical of the conclusions drawn by Prof. M.N. Srinivas in his book on the Kodavas. Veena says she was disturbed by the book "because I felt the book gazed at the Kodavas as if they were specimens under a microscope."

She opines: "What I found objectionable was the ways by which his own caste location as a Brahmin coloured his view of Coorg society and religion. In my view, although moulded by several strands of cultural influences, Coorg culture is unique. It was a culture that did not acknowledge the ritual superiority of the Brahmin priests."

In her article 'In Search of Meaning – a Pilgrimage to Malethirke Forest Shrine' Veena says: "The religious practices of the Kodavas are broadly located within the Hindu fold and yet they are different. They do not follow any of the religious prescriptions that govern the lives of mainstream Hindu communities."

Maj Gen Codanda K. Karumbaya, Sena Medal (Retd), who has written extensively on matters relating to Kodavas, has called for imbibing the spirit of the original Kodava tribal faith, which considered Nature as their God and ancestors as their gurus (teachers).

General Karumbaya has put forth his views on Kodava religion boldly, without trying to be politically correct. His views are stated bluntly, and he calls for a scientific approach to Kodava religion. The General notes: "In order that Kodavas emerge as a progressive community of the future with a scientific temper, I request our community members to recognize the merits of our original religion bequeathed to us by our early ancestors and discard all those false beliefs acquired from the followers of 'religions of fear' and 'social religions' with whom our destiny got entangled."

Mookonda Nitin Kushalappa, author of two books on Kodagu, opines that Kodavas at present largely identify themselves as Hindus, almost by default, since they do not belong to any of the other major religions in India.

Nitin states: "I would like to state that the Kodavas are presently like the mainstream Hindus in some ways and unlike them in other ways. In other words, they definitely follow a distinct way of life which is, however, not completely unrelated to Hinduism. Whether we, Kodavas, call ourselves a sect of Hindus – Kodava Hindus, or followers of an independent Kodava religion is actually a question of perception and therefore of how we label ourselves."

Roona Uthappa Ballachanda says that modern, urbanized, liberated Kodavas are increasingly clueless about how to maintain their Kodava self in the face of all the enticing new concepts around them and the gradual loss of their traditional lifestyle. "If we don't have a strong sense of self, if we don't take the time to spell out what makes us who we are and what is important to our identity, we won't be able to protect ourselves against external influence and aggression. And if the Kodava is destroyed, Kodagu will follow soon enough", notes Roona.

Under these circumstances, she argues that a religious minority status for Kodavas would give us a "strong leg to stand on, both in legal battles as well as in community endeavors."

Getting independent parliamentary representation and

full minority status for Kodavas under Article 29 of the Constitution is the road ahead for Kodavas to maintain their culture and way of life.

In their foreword to the book, researchers Boverianda Chinnappa and Nanjamma Chinnappa have called upon Kodavas to imbibe the spirit of 'Kodavame', or the Kodava way of life, a precious heritage handed down by their ancestors. "We hope that it will be practiced and preserved for generations to come, and continue to add to the rich diversity of faiths in India," say the Chinnappa couple, who have gone through the manuscript of this book and offered valuable suggestions.

I have always believed that a good cover design is important for a book. The cover for my last book, the international award-winning 'The Romance of Indian Coffee', was designed by my young friend Franz Mendonsa, who has a Master's in Entertainment Technology from Carnegie Mellon University. This time too, I roped in Mangaluru-born Franz, who currently resides in the United States and works on the Star Wars franchise.

P.T. Bopanna

Nadikerianda ainmane in Karada.

Nadikerianda kaimada in Karada.

Ancestor images in wood. Kanganda kaimada in Napoklu.

Photos by Boverianda Chinnappa

Researchers Boverianda Nanjamma Chinnappa and Boverianda Chinnappa.

Boverianda Chinnappa is an Engineer with degrees from Guindy, Madras University and Northwestern University, USA. Nanjamma Chinnappa is a Statistician with degrees from Madras University and the Indian Statistical Institute, and an honorary Doctorate from Mangalore University. She was a Visiting Fellow at Cambridge University, UK. After pursuing their careers in various capacities in India and Canada, they returned to India on retirement.

The couple then dedicated themselves to the documentation of Kodava culture. Their English translation of the 'Pattole Palame' (1924) by their common grandfather Nadikerianda Chinnappa, was published in 2003. Their second book, 'Ainmanes of Kodagu', on the ancestral homes in Kodagu, was published in 2014. They are currently working on a web-site www.ainmanes.com that contains information and photographs of the nearly 800 ainmanes covered in the field-work for their book on ainmanes.

FOREWORD

DR.BOVERIANDA NANJAMMA CHINNAPPA AND BOVERIANDA CHINNAPPA

We commend P.T.Bopanna for his initiative in selecting the theme for this book and bringing together well-known writers to contribute to it – a book whose time has come. This book may well be the catalyst that will help Kodavas understand and appreciate their way of life and take steps to preserve it.

The title of this book 'Are Kodavas(Coorgs) Hindus?' is undoubtedly thought-provoking. It is an important question for today's Kodavas to ponder upon – a question that may not even occur to most of them. While seeking to answer it, this book attempts to understand the question, discusses it from various points of view, and introspects on 'Kodavame', the way of life of the Kodava community.

Kodavas are an ancient tribe, who were primarily ancestor and nature worshippers. Like most primitive tribes, they deified their ancestors; they respected the forces of nature that governed their lives, and worshipped the deities who they believed embodied or controlled each of these forces.

Hinduism is an ancient religion that evolved over a long period of time. It is more a spiritual way of life than an organized religion. Unlike the other major religions,

Hinduism has no one holy text that defines it but a multitude of sacred writings that cover a whole range of beliefs. Amongst its countless gods are the tribal deities who were absorbed into the Hindu pantheon.

Over time, with the spread of Hinduism in South India, Kodavas, like other tribal groups, assimilated some of the Hindu beliefs and forms of worship, although they did not accept Brahmins in their rituals or adopt the caste system of Hinduism. Their deities too were absorbed into the Hindu pantheon.

The articles in this well-researched and informative book address the question posed in the title from the points of view of several writers – views that overlap, converge, diverge and sometimes are quite different from each other. The writers have defined the key words in the title, or words related to it – 'Kodavas', 'Hindus' and 'religion' – in order to clarify and elaborate their views. They have pointed out the stark differences between some of the Kodava customs and those followed by Hindus and have shown how, over time, the Kodava way of life has moved towards the Hindu way of life. And, in order to give some context to the question, they have described Kodava customs and practices and narrated its history in brief.

The author of the book, P.T.Bopanna, says this is "a serious effort...to analyze and debate the various facets of Kodava religion" and "to inform Kodavas, especially the younger generation, about their original faith and belief system" and "help them to better appreciate their original faith which is slowly being eroded...."

That raises another question – why is it important that Kodavas be made aware of and appreciate their original faith? This has been answered in different ways by the writers and may be summed up as: so that they are inspired to maintain their unique identity and faith which respects elders and nature and which keeps their society stable and helps protect the environment. One may further ask – but why is it important to practice and preserve this unique identity and faith? To which, the answer in this book is: because it adds to the diversity and richness of global culture and helps it survive, just as the variety of species in nature adds to the rich biodiversity of life on earth and helps it survive.

We wish to add another dimension to this answer: The immensely practical and pragmatic nature of Kodava customs made them easy to comply with. Because the codes of conduct and traditions of Kodava faith were transmitted orally down generations, with no 'guru' or 'dogmatic document' to dictate customs, they were not frozen in time, and remained flexible enough to meet the needs of changing circumstances.

In the words of Dr. Sarvepalli Radhakishnan: "It is essential to every religion that its heritage should be treated as sacred" to help "transmit culture and ensure the continuity of civilization."…"A living tradition influences our inner faculties, humanizes our nature, and lifts us up to a higher level. By means of it, every generation is moulded in a particular cast which gives individuality and interest to every cultural type."

The writers Bopanna chose for the book, as their articles

reveal, have themselves lived the Kodava way of life, have observed Kodava cultural practices keenly, studied them, thought deeply about them and questioned them. They have written honestly, boldly, forcefully, and with conviction. Each writer wrote from his or her perspective, unaware of what the other contributions to the book would be, and that has added to the value of the book as a text to be debated.

We urge Kodavas to read this book attentively, debate and discuss the views presented in it, especially the 'way forward' suggested at the end. And, at a personal level, we encourage them to understand and practice the simple, unique faith of the Kodavas with pride. Kodavame is a precious heritage handed down to us Kodavas by our ancestors. We hope that it will be practiced and preserved for generations to come, and continue to add to the rich diversity of faiths in India.

Dr. Chotteyandamada Sowmya Dechamma

is an Associate Professor at the Centre for Comparative Literature, University of Hyderabad. Apart from teaching Comparative Indian Literature and Cultural Discourses in Contemporary India, her research interests include Minority Discourse and Kodava Language and Culture.

She has visited the University of California, Santa Cruz as a Visiting Scholar in 2005. She was a Commonwealth Fellow at the University of Southampton during September 2010 – March 2011, and was awarded the Indo-Hungarian Education Exchange Programme for teachers during 2010. She has co-edited a book titled Cinemas of South India: Culture, Resistance, Ideology,

2010, published by Oxford University Press and has published articles in various journals.

ARE KODAVAS HINDUS?

DR.SOWMYA DECHAMMA

Are Kodavas Hindus? This at one level is a rhetorical question to which answers can be multiple and contradicting. For me, this question raises several other connected and important questions. Why does this question come up again and again in the public and private domains of Kodava lives? This question is not new. It has always been present in one form or the other from the times of colonial ethnographers/administrators like Rev. Moegling, Rev. G. Richter and Lewis Rice, who documented the lives of Kodavas, to the times of Indian Sociologists such as M. N.Srinivas.

While it was essentially outsiders who discussed this issue in the past, since the last twenty-five years or so, it is we Kodavas who raise this question and discuss and debate it amongst ourselves. The fact that the question of Kodava religion continues to be alive gives credence to the issue and shows that it is still relevant.

This write-up therefore only seeks to extend and add to the debate. Some issues raised here have already been raised in the past. Nevertheless, for purposes of clarity and argument, I make them again, substantiating them from my own observations and those of others.

Let me also point out that this question of whether a particular community belongs to a particular religion is not at all new and is not specific to Kodavas alone. The first person known to have raised this issue was Bertrand Russell, the famous British Philosopher and writer who gave a talk "Why I am not a Christian" in 1927, which later came out as a book. Much later in 1995, Ibn Warraq, wrote the book "Why I am not a Muslim".

Almost around the same time, Kancha Ilaiah, intellectual and sociologist from Telangana wrote the now famous "Why I am not a Hindu" in 1996. Tracing his community practices to the shepherd caste he belongs to, Ilaiah made a compelling argument as to why 'backward castes' and Dalits cannot be considered as belonging to the Hindu fold. In fact, this debate as to whether 'untouchables'/Dalits are Hindus or not was/is a fiercely contested one since the times of Gandhi who systematically produced a discourse around the issue[1].

It is useful to have some basic understanding of religion itself before we come to the term Hindu. How do we understand religion? In very broad terms, every religion is supposed to express a unique set of values. Around the world, a broad classification of religions is based on Semitism (descendants of Shem, son of Prophet Noah, which includes Christianity, Islam and Judaism) and non-Semitism (which includes all other religions of the world). Each of the Semitic religions is based on a single book, while the non-semitic ones are not.

1. 1. See Nathaniel Roberts book 'To be Cared for: The Power of Conversion and Foreignness of Belonging in an Indian Slum, Navayana', New Delhi, 2016, pages 111 to 151, for these debates involving Gandhi and Untouchables.

In fact, since the early colonisers did not comprehend the religions of the East, they came up with books for those religions which did not have any: the Bhagavad Gita for 'Hindus', the Tripitaka for Buddhists and such. That Brahmin men and aristocrats were the only ones allowed to learn and read Sanskrit and that the Gita, written in Sanskrit, never formed a part of the day-to-day life of Hindus says enough about how the Gita was constructed as the holy book only much later on in history.

It is by now well known that the word 'Hindu' does not belong to Sanskrit or the Dravidian languages or to any other languages of India. It is a Persian term used to refer to people beyond the 'Sindhu' river and never referred to a people belonging to a particular religion until the medieval times. It was with the Europeans crossing the sea and coming east that they started classifying people, categorising them into knowable, controllable units – be it religion, caste, region, language, or otherwise.

Scholars like James Scott have very impressively pointed out how the colonial rulers and later the modern nation state have always desired to rule by categorising and by legitimising unknown things/people using various methods[2]. This is best manifest in the census which

2. . See for more details -- Scott, James. 1998. 'Seeing Like a State: How Certain Schemes to Improve the Human Condition Have Failed'. New Haven: Yale University Press and James Scott, John Tehranian and Jeremy Mathias. 2002. The production of legal identities proper to states: The case of the permanent

began in India under the British colonial rule in 1871 which categorised all kinds of people under a particular religion, language, caste, or tribe even though they did not belong to that category, simply because the group they belonged to was a small one that was unknown or had not been categorised. And most often, such small groups were clubbed with the majority category.

Thus, not only Kodavas but many other small communities got classified as Hindu even as Census officials noted and recorded the distinct practices of these communities. Justifiably, post-colonial cultures have questioned the means and methods that were used by the colonisers to understand the varied cultures in India and in other countries. How can people belonging to other cultures define and categorise us – is the question that has bothered post-colonial cultures. Extending this, Kodavas (or any other community) can also ask – can others interpret, analyse, and define us better than ourselves? How has our own understanding of ourselves been shaped by our interaction with others?

In order to ask the question 'Are Kodavas Hindus?' we first need to ask – what is Hinduism? It has already been noted that Hinduism first came to being as a term used for people living beyond the Sindhu river and not as belonging to any religion. This later on took the colour of religion. What are the central features of Hinduism? From the known, recorded times, the Brahmin caste

family surname. Comparative Studies in Society and History, 44 (1): 4-44.

system has been one of the defining features of Hinduism, the other being idol worship.

What is the Kodava relationship with caste? I would argue that Kodavas do not belong to the caste system that is prescribed and practiced by Hindus. One important factor that characterises this caste system is the belief in the ritual supremacy of Brahmins.

The non-involvement of Brahmins in any of the rituals or ceremonies of Kodavas is common knowledge to all Kodavas. Among Kodavas, it is the elders who conduct all auspicious and not-so-auspicious rituals, whereas for all Hindu castes, it is only the presence of a Brahmin that sanctifies any ritual, since it is believed that only he can mediate between humans and their supreme beings.

This brings us to the question of Kodava gods. Like many small religions, neither Kodava folklore nor their practices refer to any one supernatural being, who is not visible to the eye, as their god. It is either the ancestral spirit Guru Karona or other spirits like Kulika that govern our cosmology. It is these spirits that we invoke in every one of our practices, day-to-day or occasional. Neither is any of the Kodava festivals based on a god. It is around our lived experiences, and around our livelihood that the festivals of Kailpod and Puthari are based, not on any god – Hindu or otherwise. Even Kaveri Sankramana, which many have noted is a recently introduced festival, revolves around a river whose tributaries are the lifeline of Kodagu.

One only needs to pay a little more attention to note that

idol worship is non-existent among Kodavas. If one looks at the place where the thook bolcha (sacred hanging lamp – that is lit daily) is kept and where all important events in the family are solemnised) or the space where meedi (offering to the ancestors) is kept, one would notice the striking emptiness of these spaces. To my knowledge, no idol or photograph adorns this space, although there are a few exceptions these days among those influenced by the popular cultures in the surrounding areas and by Hinduism in particular. This is also true for kaimadas (ancestral shrines) which perhaps were central to our worship of ancestors, now reduced to an annual affair during the Karonang Kodpo ritual. Most kaimadas are open and empty except for an oil wick lamp. Occasionally, in some kaimadas, one finds figurines vaguely resembling humans placed there to symbolize ancestors male or female – although even this distinction is not clear in the stone figures. Renovated kaimadas these days sometimes flaunt the picture of a Hindu god in the wall tiles used, but the space for worship is essentially open and empty with no idols of any god.

What this means to me is that for Kodavas, the relationship between ancestors and the living is direct, unmediated by anyone. Our ancestors are as much a part of us as we are part of them. It is only in the last two decades or so that in a few Kodava houses of nuclear families one sees a separate room for Hindu gods. None of the older houses or ancestral homes has such a room set apart for prayer to gods. On the other hand, the ainmanes or ancestral homes of Kodavas have a kanni kombare, a room set apart as sacred to their ancestors, to pray and make ritual offerings to them. Also to be noted is the fact that Kodavas make animal sacrifices and liquor offerings to spirits such as Kulika, and to their ancestors in the usual meedi offerings. They offer whatever they have for their meal that day to their ancestors – from pork to vegetables to water to liquor. This does not fall under the rigid notions of 'purity' and 'pollution' that defines Hinduism and its caste practices.

In caste Hindu practices, although some castes do eat meat and savour liquor, offering them to gods is not done since such offerings are considered to be essentially impure. Neither do caste Hindus eat meat or have liquor during any of their festivals, unlike Kodavas. Some do, but not on the main day of the festival.

That begs the question – do Kodavas belong to any of the Hindu castes? One popular claim is that Kodavas are Kshatriyas or the warrior caste, the second in the hierarchy of the Hindu caste system. This is a claim that many of the shudra castes too have made in recent times. How do we understand this?

A little history of the common perception of a Kodava and a Kodava man's physique: in the popular memory of both Kodavas and Kannadigas, Kodava men are thought of as warriors and this automatically leads to the assumption that they belong to the warrior caste. This misconstrued warrior identity is because of the supposedly good martial skills of Kodava men who 'served' under the kings who ruled Kodagu. Although the geographical and political entity of Kodagu has been changing over time and under different rulers, Kodagu has never been ruled by an 'insider', a Kodava. We are organised in terms of clans and have clan heads, like most tribal communities of the world. Interestingly, Kodagu has always been ruled by 'outsiders' including the Lingayat kings who made Madikeri their seat of power and ruled over Kodagu for over 200 years. The people of Kodagu have been smallscale agriculturists with hunting and gathering supplementing subsistence farming, until the arrival of coffee plantations with the British. As to their physique, as in any thickly-forested hilly terrain with harsh climatic conditions, the people of Kodagu adopted means of survival that made their minds and bodies sturdy and best suited to rigour.

From the well-documented times of Lingayat kings (1600– 1834), Kodavas have at best been dewans, and mostly foot soldiers for the king. Despite being outside the framework of the Hindu caste system, the ruling powers have always found it convenient to bracket Kodavas as Hindu warriors for purposes that are obvious – to be used as soldiers and to consolidate their power against the enemy both from 'outside' and from 'within' Kodagu.

In addition, the Lingayat kings had a system of hittibitti chakri, a system that almost amounted to bonded labour. Under this hittibitti chakri system, every family in Kodagu, Kodava or otherwise, had to work for the king as a soldier, as a guard, or do any other job ordered by the king. And, like all monarchs, the Lingayat kings punished those not complying with this decree, death being the severest punishment. This hittibitti chakri forced some Kodavas to take up arms and volunteer as soldiers, gradually adding to the notion of Kodavas as warriors.

This notion of Kodavas as warriors was also concretized by the colonial government, which exempted the jamma landholders of Kodagu from the Indian Arms Acts of 1861, 1878, and 1924 so as to use their services in Kodagu where there was no regular military or police force then. This exemption continues even today, making the possession of arms much easier for all jamma land holders of Kodagu. So the gun-wielding Kodava man has become 'the image' of Kodavas.

The colonial discourse that was prevalent in the late Victorian and early twentieth century also added to this history of 'Kodava as warrior'. Very many Kodavas have also bought this theory of Kodavas belonging to a martial/warrior race. This has resulted in the Kodava symbol consisting of the peeche kathi (a dagger tucked into the sash of the traditional dress of a Kodava man), odi kathi (a broad-bladed sword) and the gun – all too obviously male warrior-like.

The myth of Kodavas as belonging to some warrior caste is not only baseless but conveniently supports M.N. Srinivas's theory of sanskritisation uncritically. That the first commander-in-chief of independent India, Field Marshall K.M. Cariappa, and Gen. K.S.Thimayya, one of the earliest army chiefs, are both Kodavas has further added to this myth.

Interestingly and contradictorily, the government of

Karnataka categorizes Kodavas, the dominant community of Kodagu, as belonging to Other Backward Classes (OBC) (III A). Since classifying of OBCs happened only after independence, grouping of people who are classified and defined as OBCs becomes very problematic.

At present there exist three prominent notions of community among the Kodavas: (1) that Kodavas are a tribe, albeit socially more mobile than other tribes; (2) that Kodavas belong to Other Backward Classes but not necessarily Hindu; (3) that Kodavas are an upwardly mobile community despite marked differences from that of the Brahminical Hindu. When a community defies definition that frames it within the Brahminical order, the state apparatus finds it convenient to 'bind it serially' in the OBC Hindu list, thereby saying that although communities such as Kodavas are 'a little different' – they eat pork for instance – but are not Christians, and are not Muslims, and therefore they are Hindus. And precisely because they are different, they need to be down in the order but not outside it; this difference needs to be assimilated into the very end of margins as a 'different Hindu' defined by the state/ hegemonic groups[3].

3. 3. This part on the (mis)construction of Kodavas as belonging to a warrior caste is taken largely from my earlier paper on "The Model Minority: Problematizing the Representation of Kodavas in Kannada Cinema", in Inter-Asia Cultural Studies, Volume 13, Issue 1, 2012 (5-21).

Patriarchy combined with caste marks another major feature of Hinduism. One of the main beliefs among caste Hindus is the desire for a son so that one could be cremated by the son and son only. This is the only way Hindus believe one will be free from this world.

If one observes the death rituals of the Kodavas, we see that the first right to light the pyre goes to the husband or wife of the deceased and then only to others.The son is seen as just another member of the family who would assist in the rituals along with the husband /wife /daughter/ parent of the deceased. That the wife can and is entitled by custom to light the pyre of her husband is something that is utterly against all norms of Hinduism.

In addition, the fact that Kodavas are buried in times of rain or when death befalls children or when the person dying or his/her family so wishes, is another pointer that shows how unlike Hindus Kodavas are. They do not have Hinduism's fixation with cremation. Kodava practices are fluid and not dogmatic. Another notable difference is that widowed Kodava women are not considered inauspicious. Following tradition, they remarry and so do women separated from their husbands, with rituals prescribed for such re-marriages – something that traditionally caste Hindus were totally against.

There are a whole lot of contentions about practices of marriage among Kodavas in pre-colonial times, but to a large extent Kodavas have been patrilineal, where landed property is inherited only by male heirs. Before the free market, and before coffee plantations expanded, there was hardly any property to distribute in Kodagu. Now, despite Kodava practices in relation to women being more democratic, there are traces of Hinduism's chauvinism creeping in, and that is a matter of concern.

One argument that supports the Hindu claim of Kodavas is the presence of temples in almost every village of Kodagu. This is not at all surprising. From the colonial times as recorded in the Archaeology of Coorg to M. N.Srinivas's Religion and Society among the Coorgs of South India, it is pointed out that almost all temples of Kodagu date from around the time of Lingayat Kings. This implies that temples, especially those dedicated to major Saivaite gods were built around that time. There are also innumerable temples of 'minor' gods like Bhagavati, Muthappan, etc.

These gods, whether Hindu or not, have "travelled" from Kerala and "came" to Kodagu over time. It is also pointed out that the presence of Tulu-speaking and Kannada-speaking Brahmins in some of these temples show that these Brahmins do not belong to Kodagu but were brought over by the Lingayat kings to establish their own religious and other interests in Kodagu. This, as we see in history, has been a device used by kings to expand their influence territorially as well as in socio-cultural terms. However, despite the presence of all these gods and more, Kodavas have quite steadfastly retained the practices of their native rituals, ceremonies and festivals and this points to the resilience of smaller religions.

Another feature that most societies, whether western or eastern, have is that of a hierarchical structure among the communities that speak the same language and inhabit the same region. This is also found in Kodagu where Kodava speakers are not just Kodavas but include Heggades, Ayiris, Hajamas, Malayas and Amma Kodavas among others. The relationship among all these communities pretty much resembles caste structures of Hinduism. What we need to remember is that this is an evil replica of the caste system outside the fold of Hinduism. But most of these communities' practices do not resemble Hindu practices.

There are hardly any relationships, may it be of inter-community marriages or other social relationships, between these communities, except for occupational ones that revolves around power of land holders (Kodavas or others). The practice of Poleyas playing drums (valaga) at almost all rituals of Kodavas points to some traces of caste Hinduism in Kodavas practices. That most Poleyas are Kannada speakers points to the possibility of them being another group which the Lingayat kings brought with them.

Let me also put this straight. There are major, dominant religions and there are small, local non-dominant religions. Not belonging to one of the major religions does not mean that one ends up belonging to another major religion. If one is not Hindu it does not mean that one is Muslim or Christian.

The best examples are from the native religions of America or Australia that have been in existence much before the white people colonised these continents. Iroquois, Pueblo, Mi'kmaq, Navajo, in Northern America, the many Aborginal tribes in Australia, and the Maoris of New-Zealand are a few among them. In the same way, religions of tribes in India, may it be Santhal, Ho in the Eastern belt, Lushai, Khasi, Angami, Bodo (and 250 others) in the North-eastern belt or our own neighbours Eravas, Kurubas – cannot be classified as Hindu just because they do not practice Christianity or Islam. Of course that we have treated them as inferior and almost like slaves in the past points to the Kodava structures that are feudal, classist.

The cosmology and ways of life of the Kodava, Erava and other 'small' religions are entirely different from those of dominant religions, and it is time we recognise 'small' religions for their own worth. Whether these religions want to call themselves simply by their own name (Navajo or Kodava or Erava) or whether these communities want to be considered as a distinct tribe is the people's own choice and to a large extent a governmental construct. There is nothing small in belonging to a small religion, especially when these smaller religions are relatively more democratic, less dogmatic and open to changes for the better. It therefore works well for the Kodavas to be Kodavas and not Hindus.

OF DEATH, RITUALS AND SONGS FOR THE DEAD: KODAVAS AND THEIR HISTORIES

DR.SOWMYA DECHAMMA

Note: This paper was published as "Of Death, Rituals and Songs for the Dead: Kodavas and their Histories" in Intersections: Gender and Sexuality in Asia and the Pacific," Issue 34, March 2014.

I begin with a personal anecdote. It was 1990–91 and, at fourteen-years old, I was in the ninth grade at high school. The school had taken us for a trek-picnic and we had hiked up a hill on the outskirts of our small town, Somwarpet, in the district of Kodagu, Karnataka State, India. Among others, we were accompanied by our history teacher who was from Mysore, the cultural capital and the scene of all 'the noteworthy' history in the State for centuries.

The view from the hilltop was magnificent and we were taking it in when the history teacher joined us and said: "You people of Kodagu have only scenic beauty to boast about and have no history at all." Fourteen years is still an age when the teacher's word is sacrosanct. This is especially so when you are trained to believe that history happens 'out there' to someone 'up there' and not for or about you, and that history is the written record of the rulers with temples, palaces, forts and monuments for witnesses.

Histories, oral or otherwise, of people like Kodavas, a minority community in terms of number, power and socio-cultural practices, are dismissed and erased during such day-to-day discourses, which is largely a result of the way in which mainstream academic discourses governed by hegemonic groups deal with history. It is only now as an adult academic that I can think of counter-arguments, of alternate histories that are much richer and enlivening than the history we are normally asked to accept unquestioningly. This paper is therefore an attempt, to listen, to retell, and to understand our own histories through narratives – oral and ritual.

My effort in this paper is to point out how death becomes central in human life and human history. And how, through the songs for the dead, a minority community offers its own version of its history that differs from dominant versions of its history. More importantly, it gives us methods of charting history, and understanding history in a way that has rarely been considered or has been considered peripheral. Despite the notion and vision of history emerging from the peripheral and marginal – I, following Nadia Seremetakis, argue that these histories are not dependent and 'are capable of denying recognition to any centre'.

What follows in this introductory section is a brief discussion of the method I followed to gather source material for this paper. In the first section, 'Death Rituals and the Kodava: Reading against the Hindu,' I briefly attempt to situate the ethnographical history of Kodavas and their socio-cultural practices in the context of their identity as an indigenous community, not belonging to the order of the Hindu.

I connect this to my focus on the rituals surrounding death which I describe in some detail. In outlining the ritual practices of a community that is somewhat less studied, I want to make it clear that my reading of these practices is concerned about and connected to the constantly changing perceptions of modernity among the Kodavas and also to the changing customs and practices of the community.

Very importantly, it is through these customs that I read a counter-culture/counter-history to the dominant Hindu culture/history that, through assimilative strategies, has gradually erased histories and practices of cultures that, by their very nature, question the ways of the Hindu.

The next two sections analyze death songs through which the community's histories are read. I explore and question the masculine and the feminine as elaborated and generalised in the Hindu-Indian context. My main concern in this section is to show how songs sung for the dead and rituals of death are indeed proof of the different gendered roles among different communities.

Unlike the much-studied caste-Hindus among whom gender roles and history are seen as very specific, exclusive, and non-interchangeable, I point towards a fluid and material world of genders that to me is possible only in the absence of Brahminical hegemony.

In the final section, I read songs sung for the dead as documents of history that record the little moments; the little stories; the lives of 'inconsequential' individuals; their work; minor and major changes in climate, that affect subsistence agricultural practices; relationships, etc.

In failing to recognise a central history that controls all histories, this documenting of little stories, I argue, counters the big history which is recorded and made available to the literate world of the powerful.

My focus here is on the Kodava community that speaks the Kodava language in Kodagu or Coorg district in Southern Karnataka, India. Since I belong to the community that I am researching, the information mentioned here and its interpretation constitute an ongoing process of my observation and understanding of my community over the past ten years or so, when I began to be conscious of 'our'/my difference from mainstream culture.

I lived with my community in the district of Kodagu, for the first twenty years of my life; the following twelve years I have spent studying, researching, and working outside Kodagu. I, like most Kodavas, 'go back' to Kodagu to attend a wedding, death/funeral, child birth and Puthari – our main festival which can loosely be translated as the harvest festival.

This switching between the rural/urban, moving back and forth, neither completely rural nor completely urban – is a cultural continuum with which Kodavas identify themselves. But being a researcher, I make it a point to spend at least two months a year at home, travelling within Kodagu district, trying to understand various subtleties that have marked us as different and also have pushed us to assimilate into the Hindu fold.

However, I want to make it very clear that being both an 'insider' and a researcher is not at all easy. This is not because being an insider lacks the 'dispassionate objectivity' that is supposedly required of the researcher, for I believe that passion and subjectivity are essential for any researcher. Being an insider was not easy because of the multiple roles I had to play – as an individual, as a member of my family, my clan, my village, and my community, as an observer, ethnographer, a fellow celebrator or mourner as and when rituals so demanded.

This is what drew me strongly to Nadia Seremetakis' book, 'The Last Word: Women, Death and Divination in Inner Mani', in which she demonstrates how being an insider is more rewarding and enriching. While observing and recording rituals of festivity, even as I participate as a fellow celebrator, is a matter of joy and does not necessarily break any ritual protocol, observing and recording rituals of death demand a far more sensitive approach.

Therefore, my memory of attending funerals from May 2003 to December 2007 – during my annual two-month visits to Kodagu and at the death of people close to me, and making notes on them much later are all central to this paper. More crucial are discussions with and interpretations of my informants, two men and two women, all of whom have passed the age of fifty, (seventy being the oldest), and many others with whom I could talk (usually someone related to me, but not necessarily) during and after the death and funeral ceremonies.

Death rituals and the Kodava: Reading against the Hindu

The Kodava speakers are minorities in the sense of being linguistic and ethnic minorities, and as minorities in relation to the caste structure.They are a group of communities that is best classified as indigenous non-Hindu, for their practices clearly point to a non-Brahminical status.

The Kodavas number little more than 100,000 and they speak a distinct Dravidian language also called Kodava Thak. They are indigenous to Kodagu, a district in the Western Ghats of Karnataka state, India. The district is scenic, surrounded by hills. It has one of the heaviest rainfalls in the country and has a pleasant climate throughout the year.

In recent times, Kodavas have dispersed all over India and are mostly concentrated in the cities of Mysore and Bangalore; and some live abroad. Kodavas maintain a strong sense of cultural and social independence. All of them used to be subsistence agriculturists and hunters, and many still are, though they have given up hunting.

In terms of everyday culture and ways of life, Kodavas are governed by their material world and are quite secular. Unlike Hindus, their religious beliefs are not embodied in permanent forms and they do not practice idol worship. They eat meat and consume liquor during all ritual occasions. They also do not worship fire, which is central to Hindu rituals, and fire does not figure in any of their traditional rituals.

Kodavas are divided into patrilineal clans called okka, with each okka having a separate kaimada (place of worship of their ancestors). They also worship agricultural and hunting tools and appease their ancestors and certain spirits (such as Kuliya) once a year.

There seems to be no central concept of god, with most god-based temples of recent origin in Kodagu being brought in from either the neighbouring Dakshina Kannada district of Karnataka or Malabar region of Kerala. Along with Kodava, the other two main languages spoken in Kodagu are Kannada and Malayalam (Kodagu borders Kerala). Again, the relationship among Kodava speakers within Kodagu and their relation to Kannada speakers within and outside Kodagu are marked not only by differences in language, but also by differences in what is generally termed as 'ethnic culture', and most importantly they are marked by caste that characterises this culture.

In the popular memory of both Kodavas and Kannadigas (including other peoples who also live in the State of Karnataka and who speak Kannada), Kodavas are thought of as warriors. This automatically leads to the assumption that they belong to the warrior caste.

This misconstrued warrior identity arose because of the supposedly good martial skills of Kodava men who 'served' under the kings who once ruled Kodagu. Though the geographical and political entity of Kodagu has changed over time and under different rulers, Kodagu has never been ruled by an 'insider' – Kodava or any others from Kodagu.

Interestingly, it has always been ruled by 'outsiders' including the kings belonging to the Lingayat caste. These kings hailed from Ikkeri, a small village near Shimoga in Karnataka, and had their seat of power initially at Haleri near Madikeri. The people of Kodagu have been small-scale agriculturists with hunting and gathering as supplements to subsistence farming until the arrival of British coffee plantations.

From the well-documented times of Haleri kings (1600–1834), Kodavas at best have been dewans and mostly foot soldiers for the king. A cursory glance at the customs and rituals of most Kodava-speaking peoples show that they are neither idol worshippers nor do they include priestly Brahmins in any of their ceremonies. All their festivals revolve around agricultural practices and none in the name of any Hindu god.

This is practiced even today to a large extent. But interestingly, the government of Karnataka categorises the Kodavas of Kodagu as belonging to 'Other Backward Classes' (OBC) which falls under the shudra/low category under the Hindu caste system, although they are a modernised indigenous group outside the fold of Hinduism.

When a community defies a definition that frames it within the Brahminical order, the state apparatus finds it convenient to 'bind it serially' in the OBC Hindu list, thereby saying that, though communities like Kodavas are 'a little different' – eating pork for instance, but are not Christians, and are not Muslims and therefore they are Hindus.

And precisely because they are different, they need to be ranked down in the order, but definitely not outside it. This now becomes a classic example of how although difference is desirable and unavoidable, these differences are not suppressed but are subordinated to the 'standard'.

Therefore, I argue that by virtue of being forced into the caste system as an OBC, that in itself becomes a point of identification as a Hindu, although this Hinduisation does not happen through rituals and practices. However, many Kodavas when asked about their religion mention it as Hindu. This is possibly because of their OBC status, and because one perceives that by not belonging to any other organised religion one necessarily belongs to Hinduism by default.

The polarisation of Hindu and Muslim in the recent decades has also pitted the Kodava against the Muslim and has strengthened the perception of Kodava as Hindu.

Therefore, I begin and end with the premise that Kodavas are a minority community whose practices do not belong to the hegemonic Hindu Brahminical fold. I have repeated this because it is important to know how such communities have been very conveniently bracketed as communities that in some way or the other, follow the 'Hindu way of life' since it is uncritically believed that 'Hinduism is nothing but a way of life'.

Through the reading of songs for the dead and rituals surrounding them, what I question is precisely this: how communities like the Kodavas, despite their autonomous religious practices, have been gradually assimilated as being Hindu, albeit of a lower caste. The study of death and related cultures offers a host of issues from which I can take off. Understanding death is inseparable from understanding history and, as Nadia Seremetakis points out, is inseparable from a people's 'cultural imagination.'

Conclusion:

I have in this paper argued that a community whose history has thus far been marginal can be looked at from various positions and that its history can be retold through different narratives. More importantly, histories – socio-cultural, political or otherwise of such communities have been peripheral precisely because, when told, they unsettle the dominant version of history.

Here, the attempt to open up this history through rituals of death and songs for the dead/songs in praise of the dead is to narrate a material history of the individual, of a people who are apparently unconcerned with the question of 'spirituality' after death.

Nowhere do the songs mention any kind of transcendental discourse or philosophise about death. This has to be noted because Brahmanic Hindu philosophy is very concerned about rebirth and philosophises the aftermath of death in a major way, the concept of heaven and hell being a small part in it.

In fact, the song for the dead urges the deceased not to be reborn. But these songs for the dead of the Kodavas not only do not mention 'the other worldly' things, but instead mention what matters in the lifetime, the materiality of living and living well, the problems, pleasures, 'small' traditions, 'small' resistances, 'small' heroics and 'smaller' histories.

Yet at other places, the song for the dead tells us about the crops that are grown, the labour that goes into agriculture, about harvesting, and the fluid gender roles that do not conform to the conventional inner/outer domain, about life-histories, histories of the community and so on.

The narrative history of the Kodavas, as interpreted here using the funeral songs and songs in praise of the dead and death rituals, is also much steeped in memory. This memory is not only the memory of the person deceased, but also the memory of a place, the memory of a community, of kinship, of work, of belief systems, etc.

As Kerwin Lee Klien suggests 'Memory can come to the

fore in an age of historiographic crisis precisely because it figures as a therapeutic alternative to historical discourse'. Memory, as expressed in oral history, performs more than a therapeutic function. It indicates a relationship between personal and collective histories. It also indicates that memory and history are deeply connected to a sense of place and how we use our past and our sense of a community and place to create a sense of our identity.

By narrativising the dead individual's history, the songs and rituals contextualise an individual's history within the history of the community. Apart from stating the obvious, that narratives – oral and ritual, and here specifically the songs and rituals for the dead – do give us a version of history, my attempt is to show how this history differs from the hegemonic understanding of history and how this history not only differs, but also actually questions notions of histories and ideologies of the dominant.

Through this, my attempt is also to point out how written cultures' recorded histories have marginal histories as supplements, as tokens to fill in the obvious gaps in their attempt to weave a single history of a nation, here that of Hindu India. This paper, like Wendy Singer's study of oral histories of a village in Bihar, addresses a 'post-modern preoccupation with demonstrating the inherent power-relations within scholarship', as well as the relative nature of all 'truths' and histories.

Prof. Neravanda Veena Poonacha

retired as Director of the Research Centre for Women's Studies, SNDT Women's University, Mumbai.

With a Ph.D. in Sociology from SNDT Women's University, she has contributed significantly to the growth of women's studies scholarship, through her research, publications and teaching.

She has been awarded research fellowships by the Australia-India Council in 2008, and by the University of British Colombia, Canada in 1997. She was a visiting faculty in the University of Regina, Canada in 2004.

Her publications include 'From the Land of a Thousand Hills: Portraits of Three Women of Coorg (Kodagu) in South India', 2002. She was awarded a PhD degree in 1991 for her thesis 'Women in Coorg Society: A Study of Status and Experiences through the Use of Proverbs, Folksongs, Oral Histories and Genealogies'.

IN SEARCH OF MEANING: A PILGRIMAGE TO MALETHIRKE FOREST SHRINE

DR. VEENA POONACHA

Located on the slopes of Soma Male peak in Kadiyatnad, Malethirke is one of the many forest shrines that dot the picturesque landscape of Kodagu. My visit to this sacred site of worship was a reminder of the ancient religious traditions of the Kodavas, who are described in 19th century ethnographic writings as a hardy mountain tribe with warlike traditions.

Historical accounts, since the 16th century, have long highlighted this aspect of their culture.2 In more recent historical memory, one can recall the contributions of soldiers like Field Marshal K. M. Cariappa, General K.S. Thimayya and scores of other unknown soldiers who have lived and died for their motherland.

This is not the history that I want to unearth. As a sociologist, my search is to understand the deeply embedded cultural ethos of the people – to unravel those aspects of their religion and cultural traditions that define the community.

What I found was a cultural ethos that celebrated the interconnectedness of all life forms – the land, the birds, animals and plants. No doubt, the religious life of any community is complex and comprises many elements. Apart from the philosophical/spiritual dimension, it includes ethical standards governing human behaviour, as well as rites/rituals related to life-cycle events of birth, marriage and death.

These different aspects of a religion are interconnected and reveal the belief system of the followers. The religious practices of the Kodavas are broadly located within the Hindu fold and yet they are different. They do not follow any of the religious prescriptions that govern the lives of mainstream Hindu communities.3

Unravelling the socio-religious practices of the Kodavas, reveals cross-cultural influences. Such processes of acculturation are inevitable and no culture or community can deny such influences. A case in point is the worship of Goddess Bhagavathi in every hamlet or village in Kodagu, indicating the influence of Kerala culture. Similarly the 17th century Omkareshwara temple in Madikeri reveals the influence of the Great Religious Traditions of Hinduism and is a latter day insertion into their religious beliefs. Undoubtedly these disparate strands of religious practices and belief systems have a long history and are now integral to the Kodava culture. I do not, however, wish to discuss cultural transmission and influences on cultural practices.

My quest was to find the essence of the Kodava religious ethos – an essence that has remained intrinsic to the culture, despite the march of time and the inevitable impact of socio-economic change. I feel that Kodava culture is defined by the symbiotic connection that they have with the land and all its flora and fauna. This connection is inevitable in a community dependent on agriculture.4 The idea of the sacredness of the land is evident, not just in the idiom of their songs and dances, but also in the depiction of the sacred through the conceptualization of forest shrines in sacred groves (devarakadu).5

These shrines, set amidst impenetrable forests on rugged mountainous terrain overlooking lush green valleys, indicate the roots of an indigenous culture that has been in existence since perhaps pre-historic times. It is a culture that is slowly disappearing as the Kodavas, succumbing to the lure of materialism, sell their land. Despite such erosion of religious beliefs, the continued existence and living worship at these forest shrines, attests to the pull of an ancient belief system. Adoration of the divine principle in the forest shrine indicates a belief in the wholeness of life and the need for human societies to co-exist with nature. It enjoins a veneration of all life forms – the birds, the plants and the animals.

Such an inclusive worldview is not unique to the Kodavas, but is characteristic of indigenous religious and cultural traditions across the world and is perhaps best encapsulated in an epistle written by Chief Seattle in 1854.6

"The air is precious to the red man. For all things share the same breath – the beasts, the trees, the man, they all share the same breath. What is man without the beasts? If all the beasts were gone, men would die from a great loneliness of spirit. For whatever happens to the beasts soon happens to man. All things are connected....whatever befalls the earth befalls the sons of earth." (cited in Knudtson and Suzuki 1992: xv).

Although separated by land and sea, the ideas expressed in the epistle encapsulate the essence of Kodava ethos. Their commitment to the ethics of caring for the earth is epitomized through the representation of the forests as sacred spaces.

The Malethirke forest shrine, like others that dot the land, is a simple open-air structure that does not boast of the architectural splendour evident in the other South Indian temples of Karnataka, Tamil Nadu or Kerala. Temples, especially in parts of Karnataka and Tamil Nadu, have a profusion of exquisite carvings, sculptures and frescoes, indicating the genius of human hands.The skill of the artists and artisans in erecting these magnificent structures fills one with awe.

Yet, would it be wrong to suggest that the representation of the sacred in anthropomorphic form (evident in the sculptures and frescoes) indicates a concept of divinity that privileges the human over all other forms of life?

Additionally, does the composition of the temple indicate a philosophy that sees salvation as attainable by transcending the natural world? In contrast, the simple forest shrines indicate a belief in the immanent divinity of nature and the interconnectedness of all life.

This sense of sacredness of the forest shrines is evocatively depicted in the description of the Malethirke shrine in 'Silent Sentinels, Traditional Architecture of Coorg'.

"The shrine does not have the formal characteristics of Kerala Dravida style, barring a linear axis and the hierarchical progression from the profane to the sacred. The approach to the deity is by a lane....The entire site is characterised by a high level of sensitivity to the landscape. The rising cliff face behind the deity, with its tall overgrown trees and filtered sunlight, brings with it a sense of scale that for many observers conveys a sense of the presence of a higher power."(2005: 113-117).

The Kodavas were hunters and agriculturists in the distant past. There is none the less a code of conduct governing both these occupations. Hunting was restricted to certain seasons and was proscribed in forests designated as devarakadus.7

Similarly, the traditional farmer approached the cultivation of the land with a sense of veneration. This reverence to nature and its bounty, a characteristic feature of indigenous communities, stands in contrast with the worldview shared by modern societies.

These societies, fuelled by rapid industrial expansion and over-utilization of natural resources, suffer a disconnect from the natural world. This worldview grows out of a mechanist conception of the earth. The conceptualization of the world as in- animate has evolved out of the progress of scientific knowledge since the 17th century.

The corollary to this belief system is the illusion that the human being is at the top of the evolutionary chain. This assumption entitles human societies to exploit the earth and its resources. In contrast, the ecologically sensitive worldview of tribal communities calls for the conservation and preservation of the natural world. It recognizes that the indiscriminate destruction of planet earth will ultimately destroy us. We need to reclaim this wisdom for our survival.

Footnotes:

1. I had the opportunity to visit the Malethirke shrine with my cousin Swaroop Appiah, and friends Alice Clark and Charles Taylor on January 3, 2017.
2. Ferista, a historian, remarks that a battalion of Kodava soldiers fought in the Battle of Talikota that marked the end of the Vijayanagara Empire (cited in Srinivas 2003)
3. The Kodava community is not classified within the caste system. Moreover there are no priests to officiate over any of their life-cycle rituals.
4. For instance, the Kaveri Purana celebrating the river goddess Kaveri and the Desakett Pat begin with an

invocation to the land (Nadikerianda Chinnappa 1924, translation 2003).

5. I need to clarify that there are other aspects of the religious and cultural traditions of the Kodavas that also reveal their cultural ethos, which I have not touched upon here. For instance, the home is a sacred space for the Kodavas, an aspect that is evident in the sacredness of the Ainmane (ancestral home). Similarly, reverence to their ancestors is also an intrinsic part of Kodava culture. It is the blessings of the ancestors that are sought at the beginning of every auspicious function. The more formal worship is centred on the worship of Igguthappa, God of Agriculture, the River Goddess Kaveri, and local deities like Aiyappa, God of the hunt, and Muthappa, the rebel God and hunter.

6. Chief Seattle was the leader of the Duwamish tribe in Washington territory who is supposed to have written this epistle when there was a move by the American state to purchase the land.

7. There are traditional sanctions against the indiscriminate use of weapons among the Kodavas. On Kail Polud festival day that marks the beginning of the hunting season, the members of each Kodava Okka (clan) take up their arms with deep veneration. The eldest member of the clan enjoins his family members to cautiously use their weapons, with these words: "Give way to the charge of a tiger. Avoid the rush of a boar. Do not provoke your foe. But should he attack, face up to him and fight. Always stand by a friend. Do not anger your king, and never forget God." (Nadikeranda Chinnappa 1924,

translation 2003)

References:

- Knudtson, Peter and Suzuki, David.Wisdom of the Elders.Stoddart: Canada. 1992. Pp. xv.
- Nadikerianda Chinnappa. (1924) Pattole Palame: Kodava Culture Folk songs and Traditions. Translated by Boverianda Nanjamma and Chinnappa (2003), New Delhi, Rupa and Co.
- Srinivas, M. N. (1952) Religion and Society among the Coorgs of South India. New Delhi, Oxford University Press.
- Somaya, Brinda et al. (2005). Silent Sentinels: Traditional Architecture of Coorg. Mumbai: Hecar Foundation. Pp. 2013-17.

ETHNOGRAPHY FROZEN IN TIME

DR. VEENA POONACHA

M.N. Srinivas: Religion and Society among the Coorgs of South India.

N. Delhi: Oxford University Press. 2003.

This reprint of M.N. Srinivas's classic Religion and Society among the Coorgs of South India, is indeed welcomed by all the students and teachers of sociology and social anthropology in India. Enriching the value of this edition is Andre Beteille's introduction in which he traces and contextualizes the intellectual influences that shaped Srinivas's arguments in the book and his ideas about Indian society as a whole.

As Beteille assesses, Religion and Society among the Coorgs, established Srinivas's reputation as an anthropologist and as a leading exponent of Indian culture. Influenced by the works of A. R. Radcliffe-Brown and E.E. Evans-Pritchard, the book adheres to rigid functionalism in understanding the role of religion in maintaining the structure of Coorg/Kodava society.

Given my social location in Coorg society, I am impressed with the rich ethnographic material that Srinivas has painted in his study. Having gone through the various sources of his data such as the Gazetteers, the 19th

Century census records, and the Pattole Palame (1924) by Nadikerianda Chinnappa in the course of my own study on women in Coorg, I appreciate his meticulous attention to ethnographic details.

To me this book represents an account that is frozen in time, at a critical juncture of colonial and post-colonial transformation. It is now over five decades since the book was first published; since then Coorg society has changed dramatically. Increasingly brought within the ambit of a pan-Indian culture, Coorg cultural practices have inexorably yielded to the forces of socio economic change. More and more members of the community have moved out of this tiny district, located on the slopes of the Western Ghats, in search of better educational and job opportunities.

Many of them have sold their share of their joint family property and no longer feel the tug of the land. The changing demographic pattern has impacted upon the okka (patri-clans) system, the cornerstone of the Coorg social structure. This is not to imply that the okka system has no relevance to the Coorg social structure today. Clan exogamy is strictly adhered to and the members of each clan return to their ancestral home to celebrate their festivals and rituals.

There are also newer forms of social and kinship bonding devised to maintain their community identity. For instance, many members of the different clans return to Coorg to participate in hockey matches organized between the clans. The ancient ainmane (ancestral home of an okka) still stands in solitary splendour amidst the paddy fields and coffee estates, and members of the okka gather there on festive occasions. But these once proud houses are desolate places as, for the most part, members of the okka no longer live there and the concept of joint ownership of property has given way to ideas of private ownership.

These changes are inevitable and I will not dwell at length on them. I do however like to mention some of my own responses to the theoretical frameworks of this study. In keeping with the sociological precepts of the times, the book maintains a fiction of an 'ethnographic present'. Consequently, there is an elision between the cultural practices that existed in the past and those that were in vogue when he wrote the book. It thus creates an image of a culture that is static, unchanging and frozen in time.

It fails to record the cataclysmic process of change that was taking place in the region. The people were generally well educated and their access to educational opportunities pre-dated the advent of the British. There are references in family histories and indigenous historical records to their social and political interactions with the neighbouring territories.

Ballads record the travels of the protagonists to the lowlands to sell their surplus grains and to buy commodities that were not locally available. These ballads invariably begin with an invocation to their land; an invocation which also indicates their awareness of being part of a larger sub-continent, Jaboomi (India).

This contact with the larger Indian community was evident during the period of Srinivas's fieldwork, as the community was increasingly seeking opportunities for education and economic growth outside the region. The study however does not adequately address the ways in which these interactions shaped the prevailing socio-cultural realities.

Sanskritization is a concept that germinated in this study. Srinivas saw sanskritization as a process by which a low caste was able to rise, in a generation or two, to a higher position in the caste hierarchy by adopting vegetarianism and teetotalism and by sanskritizing its rituals and pantheon. He suggests that the lower castes tend to imitate the customs and rituals of the topmost caste and that this was responsible for the spread of sanskritization. Srinivas viewed the Coorgs as a group attempting to rise in its caste status by sanskritizing their worship and way of life (Pp.30-37).

My contention is that, while it is necessary to acknowledge the process of acculturation, one can question whether the process (as applicable to the Coorgs) could be seen as sanskritization. The Coorgs were the dominant group in the region. In contrast, the Brahmins in Coorg did not wield any kind of economic, political or religious power. The Brahminical temples were (and continue to be even to this day) under the control of the Coorgs, known as deva thakka (temple headmen). Further, there is no evidence that the Coorgs ever attempted to change their dietary habits or their way of life.

Srinivas also argues that the Coorgs claim to be Kshatriyas, ranking only next to the Brahmins in the caste hierarchy – a claim that is not acceded to in the Brahminical sources. To substantiate his point, Srinivas cites the Kaveri Purana wherein the Coorgs are described as Ugras, the off-springs of a Kshatriya father and a Shudra mother. To Srinivas, the Puranas had two-fold functions: On the one hand, they absorbed local myths and legends and weaved myths around historical characters; on the other, they brought purely local myths into the mainstream. Thus, he argues, "through the purnanas, a local community becomes acquainted with the mythology of all-India Hinduism, and also its myths and legends are Sanskritized and made the property of Hindus all over India." (P. 221)

Srinivas, however, fails to sufficiently interrogate the Brahminical roots of the Kaveri Purana. An equally careful examination of the extant indigenous religious songs or the ballads of the pre-colonial period or the local versions of the Kaveri myth would have revealed that nowhere have the Coorgs claimed Kshatriya status. To inverse Srinivas's position – to an earlier interpretation of the role of the Kaveri Purana given by Richter (1870: 216-217)-it would appear that the Purana was an attempt by the Brahmin elite to bring the untamable Coorgs within a socio-political order that recognizes Brahmin dominance.

Richter writes: 'The Coorgs, it would appear, never troubled themselves much with the contents and the admonitions of the Kaveri book, and, though the translation of it was designed to make it accessible to them, it is so highly spiced with Sanscrit and old Canarese expressions, that few do understand it.' (P.217)

The Brahmins have no role to play in any of the life cycle rituals of birth, marriage and death of the Coorgs; nor are they included in any capacity during the celebrations of their festivals. The 19th century gazetteers describe the Coorgs as a distinct group who did not necessarily subscribe to the norms of Brahminical Hinduism. Rice writes that the essential feature of the Coorg religion was the non-inclusion of the Brahmins (1878:246); it comprised ancestral and demon worship (Moegling 1855 12-13; Rice 1878:257).

It is true that the gazetteers use the term caste interchangeably with tribe and community. The Coorgs (as evident from the indigenous records) however do not necessarily see themselves as a caste; nor did they claim Kshatriya status. This proves to be a technical difficulty while dealing with a larger caste-obsessed society. To avoid elaborate explanations it sometimes seems to be simpler (in view of their cultural practices and martial traditions) to describe themselves as Kshatriyas. Srinivas's attempt to fit his ethnographic data within a procrustean framework reveals his own social location as a Brahmin, for, he writes: 'The greatness of Sanskrit literature and the vitality of Indian philosophical thought in Sanskrit have also contributed to the increasing importance of Sanskritic Hinduism' (P. 219). Further he writes: 'Splinter groups like the Amma Coorgs are decades, if not centuries, in advance of their parent-groups: the former have solved their problem by Sanskritizing their customs entirely while the latter are more conservative. Sometimes the splinter groups are so far in advance of their neighbours that they incur the wrath of everyone.' (P.167)

Some of Srinivas's observations regarding the norms of pollution/ purity (pole / madi) governing the social structure are not substantiated by the ethnographic data. The Coorgs, as described by Srinivas, undoubtedly observed birth and death pollutions; but these concepts of pollution and purity were not applicable to their modes of dealing with the other castes and tribes in the region. Yet, if one were to examine the folk literature and indigenous accounts of their culture, one gets a totally different picture of Coorg culture. In the pre-colonial ballads, the mistress of the house was personally responsible for the well-being of the agricultural workers attached to the household. The mistress provided the Poliya servant packed food when he went to graze the cattle. On his return the mistress comes out of the house and pours oil on his head so that he would feel refreshed. This practice is also described in the Puthari (harvest) song and there is a proverb (palanjol) that describes the Poliya servant as equal in worth to the first son of the house.

Similarly an examination of the Coorg cultural metaphors of celebrations emphasizes notions of respect and honour. Coorg weddings, for instance, become occasions to assert kinship and village solidarity. It is an occasion for the members of the Coorg household to show their respect to their affines, their neighbours and those who work for them. For instance, the Poliya servants have the right to play the music during Kodava weddings. These servants however will only commence beating the kettle-drums and blowing the musical horns after they receive dakshina (ritual offering of betel leaf, arecanut, coconut and puffed rice along with a token sum of money to show respect) from the elders of the family. Similarly the artisans who are required to offer certain ritual services at the wedding will do so after they are offered (apart from a payment for their services) respect and dakshina. The Coorgs also had no qualms about participating in the festivals and rituals of the Poliyas, just as they visited and maintained temples of the Hindu pantheon. Therefore, it is wrong to assume (as Srinivas does) that the ritual concepts of madi/pole are related to the social structure and that a member of a high caste is in a condition of madi in relation to a member of a low caste or that the latter is in a condition of pole in relation to the former or that there is a ban on contact between castes belonging to different strata (P.109).

This is not to suggest that there was no discrimination or economic oppression of the weaker sections of the region. But rather to suggest that these discriminatory practices did not take the form of the ritualized pollution/purity norms that were systematized in Malabar, as suggested by Srinivas.

Further, describing the impact of sanskritization on gender relationships, Srinivas suggests that, on the one hand, it strengthened the conjugal bond and on the other lowered women's status in the conjugal family. This interpretation of the process of sanskritization on conjugal relationships can also be called to question: for an examination of the wedding songs and the variety of nuptial contracts (sammanda kodpa) reveals a preference for self-choice marriages (gandharva vivaha) and the absence of kanyadhan (the idea of the gift of a virgin) in marriage. Similarly, the conjugal bond is also emphasized in the funeral rites. In contrast with the Hindu custom of the son lighting the funeral pyre of his father, it is the widow who performs this funeral rite.

The point being emphasized here is that there could be multiple ways of reading ethnographic material. Srinivas's theoretical contribution is that he indicated through his study that the acculturation of cultural traits is not random but is linked to the mediation of power, prestige and status by a group with reference to the larger social structure. Srinivas emphasized the social function of religion in his Coorg study.

His own Brahminical background made him impute ritual significance to customs that are just aimed at maintaining social cohesion. Given my social location as a member of the community (although living outside Coorg) I tend to empathize more closely with the culture and the people. Therefore reading Srinivas's interpretation of my culture makes me feel objectified and showcased as some exotic plant, animal or thing. To my mind Coorg culture (despite its uniqueness in South India) is not the mirror image of other communities in the region, but rather a continuum of the Kerala, South Canara and Mysore cultures.

References

1. Chinnappa, Nadikerianda. Pattole Palame. 1924.
2. Moegling, H. Coorg Memoirs, An Account of Coorg and of the Coorg Mission. 1855. Pp. 12-13.
3. Richter G. Gazetteer of Coorg: Natural Features of the Country and the Social and Political Conditions of its Inhabitants. 1870.

SANSKRITIZATION: FAULTY INTERPRETATION OF KODAVA CULTURE BY PROF. M.N. SRINIVAS?

DR. VEENA POONACHA

Background of Ethnography Frozen in Time

My review essay, 'Ethnography Frozen in Time,' written in 2003, for the Economic and Political Weekly was born out of my discomfort with Prof. M. N. Srinivas's book Religion and Society among the Coorgs of South India. This book, first written in 1952 and reprinted in 2003, with a fresh introduction from Andre Beteille, is considered a sociological classic. Yet, it was a book which disturbed me deeply, when I first read it, as a post-graduate student of sociology. The reason why the book disturbed me was because I felt the book gazed at the Coorgs/Kodavas, as if they were specimens under a microscope.

I felt Srinivas's interpretation of Coorg culture was not the culture I knew. As a child born to Coorg parents, I presumed I knew the culture I grew up in. It was a culture that did not recognize the ritual authority of the Brahmin priest; the various Coorg rites associated with birth, marriage and death are conducted without an officiating priest. Yet, here was a sociologist who argued that the Coorgs sought to rise in the caste hierarchy by adopting certain Brahminical values, through a process he called 'sanskritization.'

I would have had no objection to his theory, if he was describing a simple process of acculturation (i.e., the process of cultural exchange and adaptation) which occurs naturally in a shared socio-cultural space. What I found objectionable was the ways by which his own caste location as a Brahmin coloured his view of Coorg society and religion. In my view, although moulded by several strands of cultural influences, Coorg culture is unique. It was a culture that did not acknowledge the ritual superiority of the Brahmin priests.

The flipside was that I decided way back in 1985 to pursue my PhD and study the Coorg cultural heritage. I was awarded a PhD degree in 1991 for my thesis Women in Coorg Society: A Study of Status and Experiences through the Use of Proverbs, Folksongs, Oral Histories and Genealogies. It was an attempt to study Coorg culture from the stand point of women's experiences.

While undertaking my thesis, I was advised by my guide, Dr.Neera Desai, an eminent sociologist, not to question Srinivas's concept of 'sanskritization,' since he was considered one of the doyens of Indian sociology. However after receiving my PhD, I have been able to present an alternative interpretation of Coorg culture within social history. It was only when the Economic and Political Weekly asked me to review his book in 2003 that I was able to voice my critique in the review.

Srinivas's interpretation of Coorg culture is still largely

unchallenged. So defining was Srinivas's work, that even writers like B.D. Ganapathy, who in the 1960s to 1980s wrote extensively on Coorg culture, did not question it. This is not to discount the importance of B.D. Ganapathy's work. I have referred to his works extensively for my thesis. I feel B.D. Ganapathy's works as well as I. M. Muthanna's works should be preserved and made available widely. It is in this context that I feel, the translation of Pattole Palame by Boverianda Nanjamma and Chinnappa into English is extremely important. It has made Nadikerianda Chinnappa's valuable work available to all scholars on Coorg. In translating this classic into English, Boverianda Nanjamma and Chinnappa have rendered yeomen service to scholars who undertake the study of the Coorgs. Many other Coorg scholars are now writing about our unique heritage, which to my mind is a positive trend.

Maj Gen Codanda K Karumbaya, SM
(Retd)

was born and educated in Madikeri, Kodagu. He was commissioned into the Army in 1958. He actively participated in the 1965 Indo-Pak war in the Rajasthan/ Sind sector, where he was wounded. In the 1971 Bangladesh war, he was awarded the Sena Medal for gallantry. He retired as Deputy Commandant of the Indian Military Academy in 1991. Maj Gen Karumbaya has written extensively on matters relating to Kodagu and contributed articles to newspapers and web portals.

KODAVAS THROUGH THE AGES

MAJ GEN CODANDA K. KARUMBAYA, SM (RETD)

Introduction

In the absence of a script of our own, our early Kodava ancestors have not been able to leave behind a record of our history or an explanation of our simple religious faith. Over a period of time, both our history and our faith have become distorted. After several centuries of our existence, we became disunited and allowed ourselves to be ruled by others. These rulers with the connivance of the priestly class, who had the ability to write, distorted our history and undermined our true faith, to serve their own interests.

Kodavas are neither Hindus, nor is our language a dialect of Kannada as we are made to believe. We are the only tribe in India without the Scheduled status, which is accorded to other tribes in India. Our customs, traditions, religious beliefs, dress and food habits are different from those of our neighbouring communities.

As our numbers are small and dwindling, we need to be given the minority status under Article 29 of the Constitution, even more deservedly than Muslims, Christians, Sikhs, Parsis and Jains. It is a fundamental duty of every citizen of the country, under Article 51A (f) of the Constitution, 'to preserve the rich heritage of our composite culture'. To brand us as Hindus, when we do not even follow their caste system, concept of gods and forms of worship, is unjust and unconstitutional.

Kodagu is as sacred to Kodavas as Mecca is to Muslims. All our Ainmanes (ancestral homes), Kaimadas (shrines dedicated to our ancestors) and Jamma lands (ancestral lands with hereditary tenure) are in Kodagu. Therefore a special provision needs to be made for Kodagu under Part XXI of the Constitution, just as was done for Jammu & Kashmir, Nagaland, Mizoram, Manipur, and Sikkim to preserve and protect our culture.

Origin of Kodavas

The story that has been repeatedly told to us, that we Kodavas are the descendants of Chandraverma, is fictitious and needs to be rejected straight away. On the other hand, among the many other theories of the origin of Kodavas, what Prof Ponjanda S. Appaiah has stated after two decades of research based on historical, anthropological and linguistic studies appears to be a plausible one.

According to Prof Appaiah, our ancestors were part of the war-like Brazani Tribe originally hailing from the Kurdish area of present-day Turkey, Iran and Iraq, which is a hilly region like Kodagu. They entered India during 320 BC in the pre-Islamic era, as a part of the Iranian contingent which had joined Emperor Alexander's invading army. In those days, when the army advanced, the families of fighting men too moved behind them, as camp followers. After Alexander turned back, some tribes in his army who had no energy to get back to their homeland, stayed back in India.

It has been established that a tribe called Drogpas migrated North along the River Indus and settled in the Kargil area for several centuries. Our ancestors, who are believed to have taken a southerly route along the Western Ghats in search of better prospects, eventually settled in Kodagu which was then an un-named, inhospitable and extremely rugged hilly region. En-route, they worked as mercenaries in different kingdoms, before the surviving twelve families, reached Baithoor in the present Kerala State, sometime during the 3rd century AD. An ancestral shrine (Kaimada) dedicated to the eldest person of this small group still exists there.

The astounding similarities between the Brazani Tribe and our own, even though separated by vast space and time, are too striking to be brushed aside by any historian. Yet, they have been ignored. Both the tribes are terraced paddy cultivators and rice is their staple food. Surprisingly, our weapons like 'Odi Kathi' and 'Piche Kathi' are similar to their weapons and have unique designs which are not found elsewhere. Our traditional dresses (especially those worn by our bride-grooms) and the folk dances of our men and women are remarkably similar to theirs. Even the jewellery worn by our women like 'KokkeThathi' and 'Pathak' have a close resemblance to theirs.

Kodagu as Homeland

After centuries of a nomadic and risky life, our ancestors

longed to have their own homeland, where they could settle down and be masters of their own destiny. The hilly region in the Western Ghats, next to Baithoor in Kerala was chosen by them as their final homeland. The word Kodagu, derived from our own Kodava language, in which 'Kodi' means 'high' and 'Adagu' means 'settlement' was an obvious and exciting choice, as the terrain was similar to what we had left behind in Kurdistan. These two words, 'Kodi' and 'Adagu' joined together became 'Kodagu'. We the original settlers of 'Kodagu' came to be called variously as 'Kodavanga', 'Kodavaru', 'Kodavas' and 'Coorgs'. The popular belief derived from Kannada literature that the word Kodagu was derived from the words 'Kroda Desha' is incorrect.

Kodagu, in those days was an inhospitable hilly region lashed with torrential rain during the monsoons. This sustained a dense forest with varieties of wild animals, birds, reptiles and insects, where no man ventured to go. Our ancestors, having been agriculturists and soldiers, knew the use of wrought iron implements. With the help of the Poleyas and the Yeravas in the neighbouring areas, who did not have a basic knowledge of agriculture and lived off the forest, our ancestors gradually moved inland, divided the land between the growing number of families and started the unique Okka system which is a way of life that is quite different from that of the Hindus.

Each Okka (patrilineal clan) had its own Ainmane and Kaimada. As Kodava women were fewer in number, some Kodava men married women from the neighbouring areas like Kerala, Dakshina Kannada

(South Canara) and Mysuru and absorbed them into our community. Braving all hardships, Kodavas gradually converted Kodagu into a prosperous region with terraced paddy fields and cultivated much sought after condiments like pepper and cardamom. They traded their produce through the sea-faring Mapillas of Malabar who became their trusted partners.

As the region prospered and security improved with the presence of Kodavas, Kodagu attracted many labourers, agriculturists, artisans, traders, and holy men from other communities in the neighbouring areas, among whom the Gowdas were prominent. Kodavas, presumably during the 15th Century AD, acquired firearms (muskets), which became as important to them as their famed Odi Kathi, and they treated their firearms with utmost reverence. The gun thereafter, played a prominent role among the Kodavas in warfare, hunting and rituals.

Kodava Faith

Kodavas do not follow any social religion that believes in Almighty Gods who are thought-reading, sin-punishing and prayer-answering interventionists. We are a simple tribal community, who consider Nature as our God. Nature is both Creator and Creation of which we are a part. It is more important to understand Nature and its manifestations such as the sun, moon, earth, water, flora, fauna and fellow human beings, so that we can live in harmony with them. We were branded as atheists, Mlechas and Kafirs, out of frustration by followers of social religions who could not understand the rationale of our faith, which is more in consonance with the astounding modern scientific discoveries. We do not have a Holy Book of our own like the Geetha, Bible or Koran. There is no such need for us, as Nature itself is our greatest book. Nature, our God, is everywhere, in everything and there is no place in the entire Universe, where there is no God.

We consider our ancestors as our Gurus (teachers) in whose memory we have built Kaimadas (ancestral shrines) near our Ainmanes (ancestral homes). Our ancestors are our role models. They believed in hard work, honesty, righteousness and family values. The right to defend ourselves against attacks from our enemies and the simple pleasure we get with our family members and friends after a hard day's work, have always been part of our ethos. Lighting a lamp in the Nellakki Nadu Bade (central hall) of our homes every morning and remembering our ancestors, gives us tremendous peace of mind and all the inspiration necessary to live our lives in a meaningful and fruitful manner. We do not need to learn the art of living from so-called 'God-men'.

Our Festivals

We have two main festivals – Kailpolud (that marks the end of the sowing season and the beginning of the hunting season) and Puthari (harvest festival), which are related to the seasons and paddy cultivation cycles. The month of Kakkada (mid-July to mid-August) is considered to be inauspicious for the simple reason that any festival in that period would interfere with the paddy transplanting work that must be done then, when the monsoon is at its heaviest and the paddy fields are full of water.

Kaveri Purana

The river Kaveri as we know it today has existed from time immemorial as a natural geographical phenomenon. The Kodavas originally called the river 'Thayoor Pole' meaning 'Motherland River', since it originated in Kodagu and flowed across our land. Being nature worshippers, we have always venerated this life-sustaining river. During the month of October, when the monsoon fury is over and the river water is in its purest form, it has been customary for Kodavas to collect water from the highest spring that feeds the river Kaveri and use it for our rituals.

The mythological story that Agastya's wife Kaveri turned into a river to serve mankind, however interesting and convincing it may seem to some, directly impinges on the Kodava belief in Nature. This river, Nature's creation, has existed for centuries, long before Agastya or the Kodavas set foot in Kodagu. Without this river, how could the copious monsoon water which the land received, drain out of Kodagu?

Kodavas must believe in truth and not continue to be fooled. The so-called 'Theerthodbhava' (annual re-birth of the river), cannot be true, as any geologist with basic knowledge can testify. It is ridiculous to claim that the river's water erupts once a year at the Kundike, the pond from where the river Kaveri takes birth, precisely on the date and at the time predicted by Hindu priests.

During the month of October in Kodagu, it is usual for bubbles to pop up in water bodies like the Kundike due to the release of air pockets in the underground vents through which the spring water emerges. Such phenomena are seen in many parts of the world. That some Kodavas still believe in Theerthodbhava, sadly exposes our submissive acceptance of what the Hindu priests tell us and our lack of scientific temper. We should worship Kaveri water in its natural form and not in a human form, that too in an alien dress. We need to restore our faith in what is true rather than placing our trust in mythological stories, written with ulterior motives.

Igguthappa Mahime

Similarly, we should be bold enough to liberate ourselves from Igguthappa Mahime (story of the glory of God Igguthappa), imposed on Kodavas by Linga Raja of the Haleri dynasty through Apparanda Bopu Diwan and the ParadandaThakkas (hereditary headmen), nominated by him, just to commemorate success in his elephant shooting expedition. Let us not forget that between this Raja, his elder brother and his son, thousands of Kodavas were killed in cold blood. Kodavas existed before Igguthappa was introduced to us and we can continue to exist, practicing the faith bequeathed to us by our Karanas (ancestors) who lived much before Linga Raja.

Blank Pages of History (3rd Century AD to 17th Century AD)

The outstanding role played by Kodavas, during the

initial 1500 years of their history in transforming Kodagu into a habitable land and a rice bowl in the region, before they came under the Rule of Haleri Rajas, has been successfully blanked out by historians, especially by those who were commissioned to write the Rajendraname and Hukum Nama by the Haleri kings. Based on some temples and inscriptions found in Kodagu, it has been ascertained that before the coming of the Haleri Rajas to Kodagu the region was ruled by the Gangas, Chalukyas, Cholas, Changalvas and Hoysalas.

Surely, these Hindu dynasties invaded Kodagu and established bases here, only to forcibly collect paddy and other farm produces as booty; but the countryside was ungovernable and was in full control of the local people. While these invading armies erected victory stones or built temples wherever they went, they hardly remained on the land and administered it. Some semblance of governance was brought about during the period of the Vijayanagara Empire that included Kodagu in the mid-14th to the mid-16th century. Nayakas, many of whom were locals, were appointed, to collect paddy and other farm produces on their behalf. The mutual rivalry between these Nayakas and the lack of unity among the Kodavas at that time sowed the seeds for our subsequent failure as a united and independent people.

Achu Nayaka's Failed Rebellion and Consolidation of the Rule of the Haleri Dynasty

In 1728 AD, Kodavas in South Kodagu, under the leadership of Achu Nayaka (belonging to the present Ajjikuttira Okka) rebelled against the then ruler, Siribai

Veerappa of the Haleri dynasty, who had gained ascendency in North Kodagu by playing one Kodava against another. The rebellion collapsed after its leader, Achu Nayaka, was treacherously ambushed and wounded near the entrance to his fort, while returning from 'Koot Bote' (a collective hunt) and then taken to the Raja as a prisoner by a Kodava Karyakara (army chief) named Paradanda Ponnappa. For this service, Ponnappa was promoted as a Diwan and vast captured property was handed over to Ponnappa's son to start a new Okka. Later, the very same Raja, got Paradanda Ponnappa killed for becoming overbearing, and subjected his family to Kuthi Nasha (destruction of the entire Paradanda Okka)! Kuthi Nasha became a powerful tool thereafter for the subsequent Rajas to subjugate the people and demand absolute obedience.

Siribai Veerappa, having thus got control of the whole of Kodagu, divided the land into 12 Kombus and 35 Nadus. He decreed that his newly acquired kingdom, Kodagu, would have one MahaThaayi (great mother, Kaveri), that each Nad (group of villages) would have a Maha Deva (God Ishwara), each Oor (village) a Povvedi (goddess Bhagavathi), each Keri (hamlet) an Ayappa (god of the hunt), each Oni (lane) a Naatha (snake god) and each Okka (clan) a Pooda (a lesser God, a spirit-deity). He then appointed 'Deva Thakkas' from gullible Kodava families to construct and run temples to these gods so as to impose Hindu beliefs on the Kodavas. This step resulted in undermining our original faith and bringing about a major distortion to it.

The practices of Kodavas consulting astrologers, performing poojas through Brahmin priests and believing in the classification of time as inauspicious (Rahu Kala) and auspicious (Gulige Kala) etc., are some of the Hindu customs which were imposed on Kodavas from this period, the 18th Century onwards.

The same Raja, also appointed Thakkas (hereditary headmen of administratve divisions) – Desha Thakkas, Seeme Thakkas, Nad Thakkas and Oor Thakkas from loyal Kodava families to administer Kodagu.

He proclaimed that all the land owned by the locals was his; but gave back the bulk of the land to the Okkas as Jamma Land with hereditary ownership and a nominal tax, under the proviso that these Okkas would, in return, supply a portion of their produce to meet the Palace requirements, agree to do Palace duties by turn and get mobilized during wars, when summoned through the Thakkas. It is ironical that the present government thinks that the Jamma lands did not belong to the locals and that the same was granted to them by the Rajas (read the government now), out of their generosity!

Achu Nayaka's failed rebellion was the turning point in the history of Kodavas, and this has not been adequately highlighted by historians. We Kodavas were effectively subjugated, made to forget our past, and serious attempts were made to undermine our faith. The Thakkas served the interest of the Rajas and not that of Kodavas. When thousands of Kodavas were killed by the last three Rajas in cold blood, these Thakkas were conspicuous by their silence. The claim that the Thakka system, which is based on loyal families appointed by the Rajas in the 18th century AD, is an original Kodava custom, is wholly wrong.

Rule of Hyder Ali and Tipu Sultan (1780 to 1791 AD)

Hyder Ali and Tipu Sultan, who became rulers of Mysore by deceit, wrested Kodagu also by force and deceit. Fuelled by their desire to carve out an empire that gave them access to ports on the west coast and to Islamise the whole population, they exterminated in cold blood many families of Kodavas who had resisted their periodic attacks. Many more, including women, were taken as prisoners, again by deceit, and forcibly converted to the Islamic faith. This was the biggest setback for Kodavas and the darkest period of our history.

Severely depleted in numbers, the Kodavas were so infuriated that not only did they rescue Vira Raja from captivity, but they also rallied under him to drive Tipu's army out of Kodagu on their own. It was only later that they rendered all help to the British, in order to eliminate Tipu Sultan once and for all. Tipu was a religious bigot and a ruthless empire builder – not the foremost freedom-fighter as made out to be by so-called historians. In order to make up their depleted numbers, Kodavas took into their fold like-minded families from other communities in Kodagu.

End of Haleri Rajas Rule (1834 AD)

Having made use of Kodavas to regain and retain their throne, the last three Rajas became increasingly cruel and autocratic. The bulk of Kodavas led by Diwans Cheppudira Ponappa and Apparanda Bopu helped the British to overthrow the last ruler, Chikka Viraraja, and bring in British rule. Kodavas also helped the British in successfully quelling the rebellion that followed, which was an attempt to bring back the rule of Haleri Rajas in Kodagu.

British Rule (1834 to 1947)

The British, no doubt exploited and ensured their colonial interests; but they were more humane and better administrators than the Haleri Rajas. Even though they treated people of all communities equally as per their merit, they trusted the Kodavas more. Many schools were started and Kodavas, who showed great interest in being educated, got better jobs and prospered. The justice system was strengthened and there was rule of law. Kodavas entered the All India services and distinguished themselves in different fields like the military, police, medicine, forest, and revenue and the true merit of Kodavas became known. The British introduced coffee cultivation in Kodagu in a big way, and coffee became a major cash crop. While they allowed Jamma tenure to continue, they started granting Jagir lands with individual ownership to those who served them well. This contributed to weakening the joint family (Okka) system that had existed for several centuries.

Kodavas, who were well versed in Kannada (the official language of the Haleri Rajas), like Appaneravanda Appacha Kavi and Nadikerianda Chinnappa started writing plays based on or documenting our history, culture, customs and traditions, in the Kodava language (using the Kannada script) and in Kannada – but unfortunately it was only as practiced by later Kodavas who had already come under the domination of the Haleri Rajas.

Even our Balo Paat (folk songs) start with the Haleri Rajas' period, and do not touch upon the earlier fourteen centuries of our history and traditions. Some of the later Kodava historians too have failed to carry out meaningful research of our glorious past, and our true faith. Sadly, with some exceptions, they have inundated us with literature that influence the younger generation and make them believe in mythologies and accept alien rituals and customs as our own.

Some recent authors have done a strategic mistake by studying the temple rituals in remote villages in Kodagu, and claiming that they are old Kodava customs which city dwellers are forgetting! Unfortunately, those villagers are more vigorous in following the imposed customs forced on us by the Deva Thakkas appointed by the Rajas during 18th/19th Centuries. It is an anomalous situation where these Brahminised Kodavas, aided and abetted by the Thakkas and modern politicians who have their own selfish agenda, are misinterpreting our original faith, and trying to convert us into Hindus! As the days pass, it will become increasingly difficult for us to revert to our earlier faith which is more in consonance with recent scientific discoveries and with universally accepted modern concepts of human behaviour.

Merger and After

After Indian independence in 1947, Coorg became an independent, centrally administered Part 'C' State. Since its merger with Karnataka in 1956, there has been a steady decline in the status of Kodagu and Kodavas. It was quite a fall from being an independent Coorg State to becoming just a small neglected district of a big State. Since its merger with Karnataka in 1956, there has been a steady decline in the status of Kodagu and Kodavas. The majority communities like Vokkaligas and Lingayats have assumed political power in Kodagu by sheer numbers and have benefitted at the cost of others. The bulk of the other non-Kodavas have been classified variously as Minorities, OBCs and SC/STs, and they are enjoying special benefits. Kannada is being imposed on Kodavas and the use of English, which is the only international/inter-state language that can fetch us good jobs, is discouraged.

Conclusion

The well-being of Kodavas and our sacred homeland, Kodagu, can only be ensured if the present misconceptions about our history and our true faith are removed. Only by this awareness can we convince ourselves and others that we are not Hindus as made out to be, but a distinct tribal community with our own language, faith, customs and traditions. Even if we are not found eligible for Scheduled Tribe status because of our comparatively better education and economic state, we are more eligible than others to earn the Minority status.

Kodavas are the original settlers of Kodagu. Kodagu and

Kodavas need Constitutional protection to preserve our unique culture and traditions. Such a step is necessary in the national interest.

ARE KODAVAS A SEPARATE RACE OR A TRIBE?

MAJ GEN CODANDA K. KARUMBAYA, SM (RETD)

I am glad that Justice (Retd) P.P. Bopanna agrees with me that Kodavas are not Hindus. He has rightly pointed out that we presently come under Hindu laws. This anomalous situation has arisen because the Union government decided to bracket small communities like Kodavas, who do not belong to any major religious group, with the majority Hindu religion, since it is impractical to have exclusive laws for every community in India, due to the large number of communities involved.

Therefore our customary laws, which were first codified by Maj. Gen. Rob Cole in 1871, have changed and are bound to change in the future also, until we have a Uniform Civil Code as envisaged in the Constitution. I consider that these changes are good for us and for the country. This decision of the government does not mean that we are Hindus and not a separate community. Under Article 25(2) of our Constitution, even bigger religious groups like Sikhs, Jains and Buddhists come under Hindu laws; but that has not prevented them from getting minority status.

As regards Justice Bopanna's contention that Kodavas are a separate 'race' and not a 'tribe', it is true that a number of early writers have referred to Kodavas as a separate 'race'. However they have also referred to Kodavas as a unique 'tribe'. For example, G Richter in his book 'The Gazetteer of Coorg' writes "The Coorgs or Kodavas as they are properly called, are the principal tribe of the country and from time immemorial, the lords of the soil............". But the same author writes elsewhere that "Coorgs are a hardy race and bear with fortitude a great deal of hardship............". Both the terms were used rather loosely by many early writers to indicate that our community is different from others in many ways.

After Independence, in pursuance of the government policy to discourage distinction between communities based on race, the 1951 Census of India did away with racial groups in India altogether. The National Census of India no longer recognises any racial group in India. Prof Ponjanda Appaiah in his book 'A History of Coorg', notes the views of the UNESCO published in 1951, that no race today can be called pure and that there is not the slightest scientific basis for considering race as a determinant of inferiority or superiority in the physical and mental capacities of people.

I have consulted a fellow Kodava, Dr Cheyanda Manu, who teaches anthropology in the University of Mysuru. He has confirmed that Kodavas are a separate tribe and not a race. Even the constitutional expert, Prof Balveer Arora has this to say: "While earlier the Kodavas referred to themselves as a distinctive race and/or nationality, a more accurate description of the Kodava people would be in terms of a linguistic and cultural community with distinctive tribal characteristics." Therefore to call ourselves as a separate race would be wrong and will not be accepted. To call ourselves boastfully as a 'martial race' is doubly wrong because there are other communities in India that are equally brave.

Some recent authors refer to Kodavas as an 'ethnic minority' meaning 'a group within a community which has different national or cultural traditions'. According to Dr B.S.Guha, a noted sociologist, the people of India are derived from six main ethnic groups, viz. Negritos, Austrics, Mongoloids, Dravidans, Western Brachycephals and Nordics. He thereafter lists various communities coming under these different ethnic groups. Coorgs and Parsis are the two communities in India who belong to Western Brachycephals. Parsis have been given minority status. Why have Kodavas not been given the same status?

A comprehensive list of tribes in India in alphabetical order is available in the website www.culturopedia.com. Kodavas are rightly included in this list and it has been correctly stated that members of the Kodava tribe live in the Kodagu region of Karnataka, which lies in the Western Ghats. I have gone through the entire list of these tribes. Out of 645 tribes in India which comprise 8.6% of the total population of India, only Kodavas have been denied scheduled status. (I request others to cross check my findings.) I feel that this decision of the government is justifiable as we Kodavas are mostly land owners with houses of our own and good education. We therefore do not meet the criteria laid down for measuring the backwardness of a community.

Armed with facts and statistics, we should convince the policy-makers that Kodavas are a rare and unique tribal community in India which needs to be given Constitutional protection. We definitely meet the criteria for earning minority status and special status for our homeland Kodagu, where our Ainmanes (ancestral homes), Kaimadas (ancestral shrines) and Jamma lands (ancestral land with hereditary tenure) are located. We have been accorded linguistic minority status (thanks to the initiative taken by some Kodava educationists) which, however, is not the same as full minority status which entitles us to many more benefits.

As of now, we Kodavas, can blame no one but ourselves for not being united in asking for our rights under the Constitution. We do not belong to the majority communities who enjoy political power, nor do we belong to those classified as minorities, and SC/STs (Scheduled Castes and Scheduled Tribes), who are privileged to get more benefits. Ordinarily Kodavas would prefer that all citizens of India are treated equally; but because Indian politics is highly communalised, that is not going to happen. This inequality has become further aggravated by the division of the country on linguistic basis in 1956.

Unfortunately, our politicians, in whom Kodavas have so far placed great faith, have failed to promote our legitimate demands as they do not want to be on the wrong side of their political masters who belong to the majority communities. Their subservient attitude and survival instincts are understandable; but some of them have been guilty of coming in the way of Kodava unity. Prof Balveer Arora in his speech at Gonikoppal, in December 2007, at the invitation of the Codava National Council, stated: "The Codavas will need to be made aware that unless they themselves claim these as distinctive markers of their identity, the efforts to seek and gain Constitutional recognition will not find adequate support in policy-making circles".

Our main drawback is that we do not have a common non-political organization based on democratic lines, where we can sit together, discuss our problems, find solutions, and project our demands in an appropriate manner.

RECOGNISE THE SUPERIORITY OF KODAVA TRIBAL FAITH AND PRESERVE IT IN ITS ORIGINAL FORM

MAJ GEN CODANDA K. KARUMBAYA, SM (RETD)

There is presently confusion among us Kodavas, as to whether we are Hindus. I feel it is wrong to call ourselves Hindus, when we do not follow the Hindu caste system, concept of Gods or forms of worship. This article aims to establish that we are a tribe, and that our Kodava tribal faith, even though very simple, is more in consonance with ongoing scientific discoveries and modern concepts of humanism. We should be proud of our faith. We consider Nature as our God and our ancestors as our gurus (teachers). We need to live in harmony with Nature and its manifestations such as the sun, moon, water, flora, fauna,and with our fellow human beings. In the evolution of human species from its primitive stage to the present and beyond, the role of religions as we know today is but a passing phase.

Humans existed before religions were thrust on them and will continue to exist even after the myths, superstitions and rituals associated with them get demolished by science in mankind's march towards the pursuit of truth. Only practices like meditation and yoga which have positive effects on the mind and body will survive while those religious beliefs that are in conflict with science will perish.

One of the greatest scientists in living memory, Albert Einstein, who too was considered to be religious, classified religions into three categories. The most primitive category was born out of fear of hunger, wild beasts, sickness and death. These are the 'religions of fear'. Later, as civilizations advanced and human societies developed, a new concept of religion took shape to impose moral conduct for the stability of society. These are the 'social religions' which invoke Gods who could reward or punish the conduct of individuals. The religions of fear and social religions do not enjoy the backing of science and cannot last long. Those who cling to them are likely to be left behind as science and technology advance at a bewildering speed.

The third category, 'Cosmic Religion', is the best of the three. Those who believe in it realize the vastness of the Universe and develop a scientific temper to try and discover its complexities. It motivates them to respect Nature and to realize the imperative need for all of us to live in harmony with it for ensuring better life in this world. Even the world has a beginning and an end, as does the Universe itself, let alone man. Albert Einstein followed this religion. Another great living scientist of our time, Stephen Hawking feels that the Universe is evolving as per some laws which may have originally been decreed by the creator who does not now intervene with its functioning. He jocularly asks – if God created the Universe, who created God? Many Hindu philosophers agree that man invented God, merely to discipline and control his own mind, which is man's most powerful attribute, not that God exists as such or as per man's perception.

Against the above background, the tenets of the original Kodava tribal faith, which considers Nature as God and our ancestors as our gurus (teachers) make it a superior form of religion. Kodavas had in the past followed oral traditions where the wisdom of our early ancestors was passed on from one generation to the next by word of mouth. Due to the lack of written accounts of Kodava history, our religion became distorted, initially by the original settlers of Kodagu and later by our rulers who established the system of Deva Thakkas to impose their religious faith on us.

At a later stage, when attempts were made to convert Kodavas into their faith by the followers of social religions like Christianity and Islam, Kodavas resisted vehemently. However it was another story as far as the Brahminical Hindu religion was concerned. The Haleri Rajas had got several Hindu temples built in different nads and villages, and appointed some Kodavas as Deva Thakkas to propagate their faith among Kodavas and to impose their Puranas which can be easily invalidated through the study of both history and science.

To this day there are many Kodavas who have immense faith in our original religion and are disdainful of other religions which are both unscientific and exploitive.

However, due to the impact of Kannada and Sanskrit literatures on Kodavas in their school curriculum and in the cultural media, and the deteriorating quality of education in the district after Kodagu merged with Karnataka (thanks to the reservation policy even in the appointment of teachers), more and more Kodavas are tending to have greater faith in alien religions at the cost of their own religion. Kodavas must get over their inferiority complex brought about by years of political and cultural subjugation. Recognizing the merits of our own religion is one of the steps to restore our confidence in ourselves.

In order that Kodavas emerge as a progressive community of the future with a scientific temper, I request our community members to recognize the merits of our original religion bequeathed to us by our early ancestors and discard all those false beliefs acquired from the followers of 'religions of fear' and 'social religions' with whom our destiny got entangled.

Recognise the Superiority of Kodava Tribal Faith and Preserve it in its Original Form.

Mookonda Nitin Kushalappa

was born in 1986 in Virajpet, Kodagu. He did his telecom engineering from CMRIT, Bengaluru. Kushalappa has authored two books on Coorg history: The Early Coorgs, 2013, and Long ago in Coorg, 2013. He writes and edits pages on Wikipedia, the online encyclopaedia, and contributes articles to newspapers. A software engineer, he has made several iPhone and iPad apps.

RELIGION AMONG THE KODAVAS

MOOKONDA NITIN KUSHALAPPA

Live long, live long, our

God, live long, Great God!

Also, live long, O Sun!

Likewise, live long, O Moon!

Earth, live long, land of our birth! 1

Before discussing the question 'Are Kodavas Hindus?' or, in other words, 'Is Kodavame a sect of Hinduism?' we need to know what is commonly understood by the terms Kodavas, Hindus, Kodavame and Hinduism. Kodavame is the way of life of the Kodavas of Kodagu, which includes their cultural and religious practices. Similarly, Hinduism is the way of life of those who claim to be Hindus, although there is no proper definition for the religion. I would opine that Kodavas, distinct in their culture and beliefs, were Hindus, or ancient Indians, by geography alone. Some of them are now, gradually, also adopting some commonly understood practices of the Hindu religion.

Tribal origins

The Kodavas, also called Coorgs, are an ethnically and

linguistically distinct people whose forefathers lived in the hilly district of Kodagu in the State of Karnataka in South India. The name of the people (Kodava) and the land (Kodagu, or Kodavu as it is known in the Kodava language) are related. It has been claimed that Kodavas are the aboriginal people of Kodagu, or Coorg.2,3 Proud of their cultural, racial, linguistic and religious identity, the Kodavas have been in South India for centuries and preceded the coming of Brahmanism, Christianity and Islam to their land.

The Kodavas are a tribe, given to agricultural and martial traditions. The Oxford dictionary describes a tribe as being: "a social division in a traditional society consisting of families or communities linked by social, economic, religious, or blood ties, with a common culture and dialect, typically having a recognised leader". The Kodavas satisfy all these criteria except that they do not have a single leader recognised by the entire community.

However Kodavas have traditionally had a council of elders who are from prominent families and are representatives of a village, naad (region, a group of villages), desha (country) or temple. They resolved legal disputes and attended to social affairs pertaining to the welfare of the people living in those geographical areas or administered the temples. This system of local governance was called thakkame and the hereditary leaders of the council were called thakkas.

But currently the use of the word 'tribe' is considered to be derogatory, since the common, but wrong, perception is that a tribe is an isolated, forest-dwelling people who gather wild plants and hunt wild creatures. The term tribe is therefore not being applied to modern Kodavas.

About the Kodavas it is said that 'as Brahminism4 made its thrust deeper into the south through the west coast, they moved out of its way to remain independent, to the region of Coorg (Kodaku/Kodagu) where in relative isolation provided by its hills, they developed as one of the advanced communities without being exploited by the Brahminic priesthood, and invaded by the caste system'. The Kodavas were 'those who digressed or moved away from the Brahminic system'5.

The Mangaraja Nighantu, a Kannada dictionary compiled in 1398, called the Kodavas Mlechchas who were given to hunting. The word Mlechcha actually means 'barbarian' or somebody who did not belong to the mainstream civilisation. It was originally used in ancient Sanskrit epic literature for 'people from the land of Melukka', which is near the Indus Valley. The mainstream civilisations, whether Indian or Western, have been demeaning the minority cultures, like the Kodava. As the adage goes, one man's religion is another man's superstition.

"Both Basava (Lingayites) and the Brahmans, however, have been unable to make much of the mountain-race of Coorg. To the present day the Coorg manages to go through life, to be born, to get his name, to marry, to die, and to have his body buried or burned, without any assistance from Brahman or Jangam (Lingayite priest).

With the exception of the religious regard paid to the cow by all India, he appears to have learned nothing from the Hinduism of the plains."6

Kodavame

The following paragraphs describe the cultural and religious practices of the Kodavas in broad terms. Every Kodava belongs to an okka (clan), which is somewhat similar to the Hindu joint family. The Kodava okka is a patrilineal one, whose members claim descent from a common ancestor going back to many generations – much like a gothra. However, while Hindus (especially Brahmins) are identified as belonging to one among seven gothras (lineages that originate with ancient sages), Kodavas belong to around a thousand okkas. An okka is identified by the okka name or mane peda, which Kodavas traditionally use in their personal names as the first initial. For instance in the Kodava Field Marshal K. M. Cariappa's name, K stands for his okka – Kodandera.

Members of the okka or clan jointly own jamma land belonging to the okka, and in the past this land was jointly occupied and tilled by the members. The jamma system of land tenure which gives permanent and hereditary right over the land to the okka is unique to Kodagu and continues to this day. The patte (title deed) of the jamma land belonging to the okka is officially recorded under the name of the current pattedara (holder of the patte), who is the male head of the okka, and inheritance of that property is along the male line of the okka. In the past, private ownership of land by individuals or nuclear families was non-existent. That, however, is common now, as in other parts of India. Jamma land itself is subdivided among members of an okka.

A married Kodava woman becomes a member of her conjugal okka, but retains her right to live in her parental ancestral home and be supported by her natal okka, should the need arise. There is no practice of dowry among Kodavas. If the marriage breaks up, custom requires that any gifts given to the bride by her parents are taken back by her. Widow re-marriage is an age-old practice and there are specific traditional rituals for such weddings. Child marriage was unknown among Kodavas even in the past, and marriages usually happened only after the age of sixteen years for both boys and girls.

Whereas among other Hindus, the groom ties the mangalasutra or thali, the sacred marital thread, around the bride's neck, among the Kodavas, the bride's mother, even if she is a widow, ties the pathak chain, the symbol of a married Kodava woman, around the bride's neck. The Hindu rituals of saptapadi and kanyadaan are not followed in Kodava weddings. The most important legally binding ritual in a Kodava wedding is sammanda kodupa conducted by elders. That is when the traditional rights of the bride in her husband's okka are enumerated in public. These rights include her right to return to her natal okka if there is a problem with the marriage.

The Kodavas have a unique institution – that of the aruva. An aruva is from a friendly neighbouring okka whose representative performs the mutually agreed role of assisting an okka in social rituals and ceremonies.

Certain places and structures, such as the mand (village green, where traditional sports, dances and feasts are held during festivals), the kaimada (shrine dedicated to ancestors), the ainmane (ancestral house of a clan), and the devakad (sacred grove) have cultural and ceremonial importance for Kodavas. A simple mud or brass lamp lit with wicks dipped in oil, representing ancestors, is prayed to in the ainmane, the kaimada and the kanni kombare (room sacred to ancestors).

Traditional Religion

Kodavas are a distinct tribe of ancestor and nature worshippers, and their ancient faith was that of reverence for their ancestors and for nature, as well as for spirit-deities, the most ancient of these being Ayyappa, god of the hunt. The Kodavas of Kodagu being a tribe, followed simple ancient rituals.

Traditionally, the local medium called the thiralakara, who is possessed by or interacts with ancestral and godly spirits while in a trance, is believed to have magical, healing and fortune-telling powers. In this respect, the indigenous beliefs of Kodavas are somewhat similar to those of their neighbours in Tulunad (Dakshina Kannada) and Malabar in North Kerala. The spirit worship ceremony, performed annually in the village temples and households, is called theray in Kodagu. In Kerala it is called theyyam while in other parts of Karnataka it is called Kola or Nema.

In Kodagu, it is said that every okka (clan) had a Puda (Bhuta, or spirit), every oni (lane) had a Nata (cobra), every keri (hamlet) had an Ayyappa (forest god), every oor (village) had a Povvadi (goddess Bhagawathi) and every nad (region comprising of a group of villages) had a Madeva (Great God, Shiva). Hence Kodavas worship spirits, snakes and a number of deities.

There were no temples or shrines in Kodagu in ancient times. A rough-hewn stone representing an ancestor or a spirit-deity, planted in a forest clearing or under a tree, served as the object of worship in those times, and still does in many parts of Kodagu. Sometimes the stone was placed on a simple platform of mud and stones that was erected in the forest clearing or built around the base of a tree. These platforms are known as tharay (or theray as it is known in some parts). The karana tharay, sacred to the karanava (ancestor), was a precursor to the kaimada; and there are tharay that are sacred to various deities (eg., Kuliya tharay dedicated to Kuliya, a spirit of the land).

Over the centuries, Kodavas have been gradually adopting the religious practices of their Hindu neighbours. Temples and shrines, mainly in the Kerala style, were built to house the gods and deities who 'came' from or were 'brought' from Kerala. Among the earliest of these was probably the Igguthappa temple in Padi, which dates from the late 12th century.

Nearly every village has a Mahadeva, a Bhadrakali or a Bhagwathi of its own, and each of these has a temple or shrine.

The Hindu deities worshipped by present day Kodavas are Madeva (Mahadeva), Padrakali (Bhadra Kali), Povvadi

(Bhagawathi), Ayyappa and Subramani (Subrahmanya). Mahadeva (Great God) is an epithet of Lord Shiva. Subramani is the elder son of Shiva and Parvathi. The remaining member of that holy family, the younger son Ganapathy, was not so prominently worshipped in Kodagu. The Ayyappa of the Kodavas is the forest-god, god of the hunt. He is not the same as HariHara puthra, the son of Shiva and Vishnu, who is revered by the Hindus, especially in Sabarimala in Kerala. Vishnu is revered as Narayana but does not have a significant place in the Kodava pantheon like the other mentioned Hindu gods. Even Vishnu's avatars, Rama and Krishna, were largely ignored among Kodavas. But Muthappa, especially Ponn-Muthappa of Parassinikadavu in Kerala, is an ancient deity of the Kodavas.

"The religion of the Coorgs consisted of ancestor and demon worship7 ; but domiciled Brahmans have introduced Mahadeva and Subrahmanya under the name of Iggutappa, and have Brahmanized the worship of the river Cauvery. The Natas, or spots on which cobras have finished their course of terrestrial life, are the objects of solemn ceremonies. Some of the banes (parcels of grazing-ground or forest) have a presiding divinity to which an annual sacrifice of pork and cakes is offered. For Ayyappa-deva are set apart extensive forests called Devara-kadu, which are untrodden by human foot and are reserved for the abodes or hunting-grounds of deified ancestors."8

Theray ceremonies

The sacred dance ritual called theray by costumed

performers dressed in the guise of a spirit-deity (such as Vishnu Murthy, Choundi, Kuttichatha, Kuliya, Muthappa and others) is performed before the shrine of that deity and is witnessed by the assembled village people. The performers who are possessed by the spirit-deity are from the Banna, Panika or Maleya communities of Kerala or from the Pale community of Tulunad. Devotees come to those possessed by the deities with offerings of chicken and/or pigs and liquor, tell them their problems and get advice from them.

This is an example of non-Brahmin spirit worship, an essential part of the local faith which came to Kodagu from neighbouring Malabar in Kerala and Tulunad in Karnataka. Theray is similar to the theyyam performances in neighbouring Malabar in Kerala and to the kola in Tulunad. This is because those regions are the origins of these spirit-deities and the practices in their shrines. The priests in these shrines are non-Brahmins. Brahmin priests do not get involved in presiding over these rituals in such shrines, as the associated deities are known to love meat. However Brahmins too visit these temples and seek the blessings of the deities.

Kodava Festivals

Kodavas have their own calendar – the solar calendar, which is the same as the Malayalam and Tamil calendars, although the month names differ. Local Kodava folk festivals are connected to their agricultural and martial traditions. These festivals are Bisu, Kakkada Padnett, Kail Polud, Kaveri Sankramana and Puthari. While they are unique since only people from Kodagu celebrate them, they are not unrelated to Hindu festivals.

Bisu, the Kodava New Year's day (called Vishu in Kerala and Vaisakhi in North India) is observed in mid-April. It is the first day of the Kodava month of Edmyaar, when the sun seems to enter the first Zodiac sign of Aries, and marks the commencement of the Kodava calendar and the agricultural cycle in Kodagu. On this day, prayers are said and oxen are yoked and made to plough the paddy fields.

The Kodava month of Kakkada, occurring during the prominence of the Cancer zodiac sign in the sky, corresponds to Ashada, Karkataka and Aadi among other South Indians and is considered to be inauspicious. Marriages and other ceremonies are not held during this month. However, transplantation of the paddy crop begins on Kakkada Padnett, the 18th day of Kakkada.

Kail Polud, which is celebrated during the Kodava month of Chingyaar, when the Simha Raasi (Leo zodiac sign) is in prominence, is the polud (auspicious time for a festival) when agricultural implements and arms are worshipped by the Kodavas, a community of agriculturists and warriors. In ancient times, this polud celebration marked the end of the paddy transplanting season and the commencement of the hunting season. Traditional agricultural implements such as ploughs and knives (that were to be put away), and hunting weapons such as war knives and long guns (that had to be readied for use), are cleaned and decorated with flowers and vermillion before being worshipped. Sports such as running races, shot-put and shooting at targets are arranged during the afternoon in the mand. All the villagers who have gathered have a hearty non-vegetarian feast that day.

Kaveri Sankramana is a festival dedicated to the river goddess Kaveri, who is the patron goddess of the Kodavas, because Kodagu is the land of her birth. It is celebrated on the first day of Tholyaar, when the sun seems to enter the Libra zodiac sign, and is the day when the river is believed to be miraculously replenished with fresh water at her source in Talakaveri. That sacred water is obtained by pilgrims who go there to witness the event, and is distributed among the natives of Kodagu. On that occasion, a decorated coconut or cucumber, symbolic of the deity Kaveri, is worshipped in Kodava homes and the families have vegetarian meals, usually comprising of dosa and pumpkin curry. This simple ritual is gradually being Hinduised, and in some homes, a kalasa, a metal pot with water inside and a coconut fitted on its rim over a crown of mango leaves and an image or a pictorial depiction of Kaveri is worshipped.

Puthari Polud is the polud for the rice harvest of Kodagu, and is dedicated to the local god Igguthappa, the god of rains and crops. It is the most important of the festivals celebrated in Kodagu, signifying the start of the rice crop harvest. It is celebrated on the night of the full moon in late November or early December, three months after the Onam (harvest) festival in Malabar, and on this day, the first sheaf of paddy is cut in the paddy fields of the okka. Puthari is celebrated over a period of many days.

Members of the okkas of all the communities in the village celebrate Puthari in their respective ainmanes or homes and then all the villagers join together in the oor mand (village green) for the Puthari kol folk dances.

An important annual ceremony of Kodavas is Karanang Kodupo (making ritual offerings to ancestors) when karanas (ancestors) are remembered by the members of the clan. This is observed on different days by different okkas. Meedi beppo (keeping ritual food) is central to this ceremony. Members of the okka gather together, pay a visit to the kekola or thutengala (graveyard or cremation ground of the okka), offer meedi (ritual food) to the deceased ancestors and relatives and later have a feast in their honour. It should be noted that in none of these festivals is there any worship of images, nor is there any role for Brahmins.

Historical Integration

The name Hindu comes from the river Sindhu, or Indus, which forms part of the western border of the Indian sub-continent. The word is of Arabic and Persian origin and of geographic importance. It was used by the Greeks to denote those living beyond the Sindhu river, i.e., those living in the sub-continent of India, a people defined by geography rather than religion. These people belonged to several sects (and not just Vedic Brahmanism9 or the later and more commonly followed ritualistic Brahminism imposed by Brahmins) in contrast to the believers of Abrahamic religions (Islam, Christianity and Judaism) who arrived from the West.

Hinduism has a pantheon of gods and goddesses, and each person is free to worship the deity of his/her choice. However, pooja (ritual worship) of these deities depicted by an image or sacred stone, whether in a house or temple, is done by Brahmin priests who recite traditional Sanskrit hymns during the pooja.

In ancient times, different sects in India worshipped different gods or deities. Many hill and forest tribes followed different gods peculiar to themselves. Gradually they appear to have accepted or been absorbed by the mainstream Hindu religion, and their gods and deities have been adopted into the Hindu pantheon of gods and deities. These days, some Kodavas keep photos or images of Hindu gods in these sacred places and pray to them as well as to their ancestors and deities.

Brahminical Supremacy

Hindus have been gradually accepting brahminical supremacy and forgetting their separate, diverse and distinct entities. Some of the Indian communities, such as the Rajputs, refused to accept Brahminical supremacy initially. But the performance of religious rites by the priests gradually made Brahmins supreme in the caste scale.

According to the Brahmins, the people of South India actually belonged to just two castes: Brahmins and Shudras. This was because the non-Brahmins of South India generally did not follow the Vedas, wear the sacred thread or hold yajnas (fire sacrifices), unlike the North Indian Kshatriyas (warriors) and Vaishyas (traders). They were therefore demeaningly labelled Shudras (working class). However the so-called Shudras of South India had a feudal system among themselves, where the kings and landlords were at the top while the landless labourers were at the bottom.

The Kodavas have resisted Brahminical supremacy over the centuries, thus retaining their native culture that they are proud of. Since they essentially rejected Brahminism as a whole, the Tulu Brahmins, who first came to Kodagu as temple priests, explained this with a local version of the Kaveri Purana. In this legend, Chandravarma, the mythical ancestor of the Kodavas who was a Kshatriya and of the Chandra vansha (lunar dynasty) conquers this land. He marries a Shudra maiden granted to him by goddess Parvathi in answer to his prayers. Their eleven sons marry the 100 princesses born to the king of Vidarbha from his Shudra wives, and, according to the legend, it is their descendants who were the progenitors of Kodavas. Chandravarma is informed that his descendants will not follow the Vedas, the holy scriptures of the Brahmins.

Brahmins who were invited by the Rajas and by prominent Kodavas to serve in the temples of Kodagu as priests did not interfere with the native Kodava customs. The earliest temple priests of Kodagu are believed to be from the local Amma community. They were superseded by Brahmin priests from Kerala. Later priests from Tulunad and other parts of Karnataka came to Kodagu. In 1870, there were 863 shrines in Kodagu, prominent among them being the Igguthappa temple in Padi, the

Omkareshwara temple in Madikeri and the Bhagandeshwara temple in Bhagamandala.

Tribes

The unique tribal culture of the 'original Hindus' (ancient Indians in this context) has now been more or less absorbed into mainstream Hinduism. The hill tribes of India had a loose hierarchy which was not as rigid as the caste system of the Hindus of the plains. These communities were inter-dependent and sometimes spoke different languages and followed different cultures, even while they lived as neighbours. In the Nilgiris, for example, the Toda were dominant, followed by the Kota, the Badaga and then the Kurumba.

In ancient Kodagu, the Kodavas co-existed with other early tribal inhabitants such as the Kudiyas, the Yeravas, the Kurubas and the Kembatti, in a similar loosely hierarchal society. The Kodavas were sedentary paddy agriculturists and militiamen. The Kudiya traditionally engaged in shifting agriculture, rather than sedentary agriculture, in the Western Ghats. While some Kudiyas spoke the Kodava language others spoke their own Kudiya language. They would also draw toddy and sometimes work as labourers. The Kuruba were wild, wandering hunter-gatherers of the forests. There were two Kuruba tribes, the honey- gathering Jenu Kuruba and the hill-dwelling Betta Kuruba. The Yeravas were nomadic labourers from Waynad. Both the Kurubas and the Yeravas had languages of their own. The Kembatti were Kodava speaking sedentary landless labourers of Kodagu. Among these indigenous people of the region, the Kodavas were the dominant tribe, being numerically larger and highest on the social ladder. They were followed by the Kudiya, the Kuruba, the Yerava and the Kembatti in that order. Many of these tribes gradually adopted the cultural practices of the Kodavas.

There were other ethnic communities in Kodagu since long ago, such as the Ammas (Amma Kodavas) and the Peggades (Kodagu Heggades) who were lesser in number and slightly different from the Kodavas. These were agricultural communities who too spoke the Kodava language and followed Kodava cultural practices. However, the Ammas, the indigenous priests of Kodagu before the advent of Brahmin priests, were vegetarians and teetotallers, and some of them began to wear the sacred thread around 1834.

Castes

Over the ages, a number of professional communities who are now identified as castes came to settle down in Kodagu. Chief among them were the Are-bhashe speaking Gowda agriculturists from Sulya. Others included the Aimbokka (Mysorean Golla or cattle breeders), the Boone patta (musical mendicants), the Banna (ceremonial oracles and spirit dancers in Kerala and Kodagu), the Airi (carpenters and ironsmiths), the Madivala (washermen), the Hajama (barbers), the Koyava (agriculturists) and the Meda (drummers, basket-makers and umbrella-makers)10.

The proud Kodavas had refused to be classified in the caste scale and had rejected Brahminical supremacy.

But, because of the influence of immigrant Brahmins, the caste system gradually made its way into Kodagu. Thus, the Kodavas themselves came to be regarded as a caste entity and to follow the Hindu caste system to some extent.

Nadikerianda Chinnappa claimed in his book, Pattole Palame written in 1924, that the Kodavas are equal in status to the Nairs of Kerala, the Bunts of Dakshina Kannada (Tulunad), the Gowda Vokkaligas of Karnataka and the Vellalas of Tamil Nadu. These mentioned castes were the landed agriculturists of South India. Since they were non-Brahmin South Indians, they were known as the high class 'Shudras'.

Next to them were the Thiyas of Kerala, the Billavas of Tulunad, the Peggades, Airis, Bannas and Madivalas of Kodagu. Hindu caste norms had historically dictated that, although they were allowed inside Kodava houses they could not enter certain areas such as the nellaki bade (central hall with the sacred lamp), the kitchen and the kanni kombare (room sacred to ancestors). After them were the Yerava, the Kuruba and the Pale (Tulu speaking labourers) who were allowed only up to the verandahs of Kodava houses. The Meda (Kodava speaking drummers and basket makers) and the Kembatti Poleya (farm hands) were allowed only up to the courtyards of the houses. However, these caste taboos are not in common practice these days.

Temple Festivals

There are a number of village temple festivals in Kodagu.

Local deities are propitiated every year when villagers gather during the respective temple festivals. The major festivals are the Boad namme (festival) and the Bhagwathi namme, associated with the Mother goddess temples. While the first is celebrated mainly in the Bhadrakali temples, the second is celebrated in the Bhagwathi temples. These happen at different times in different village temples. Temple observances for the festival begin with a stringent period called pattani, when a number of foods, including those cooked in oil, using coconuts or meat, and certain common activities, such as cutting coconuts within the house, are prohibited.

Boad namme is a boisterous festival unique to Kodagu. Every year during the months of April and May different villages in Kodagu celebrate this interesting festival. Usually these celebrations are associated with the shrines of goddess Bhadrakali or Bhagwathi.

During Boad namme, boys and men paint their bodies and wear various guises and go prancing around the village hurling abuse at their masters and even at the gods, all in fun. Accompanied by musicians who mostly play percussion instruments, they masquerade going from house to house in the village and bring vehicles on the roads that they go by to a brief pause demanding money from them, during that night and the following day.

Apart from these guised dance performers, folk singers also go to the houses in the village during Boad namme and sing the mane paat, the song of the okka, in praise of the resident family visited, as they strike on hour-glass-shaped drums called dudi with sticks. These songs are called dudi paat. Some singers carry large drums called the dol and sing what is known as the dol paat as they go from house to house.

Eventually, the villagers gather at the centre of the village, often in a temple, and all the performers gather and circumambulate the temple. A theray is organised at the shrine, and the theray dancers emulate spirit-deities as they prance around.

On one of the days of the festival, boys wearing horse-shaped cane frames participate in races called kudure aat. Also, either on that day or the next, younger boys dressed as women are led into the temple yard where a pooja is held. All these boys represent the different hamlets associated with the temple.

The Bhagwathi namme is a good example where Brahminism meets Kodavame, the Kodava lifestyle. During the days of the festival, every morning and evening, dance and song programmes are organised in the name of the goddess, and the temple walls are decorated with mud lamps lit with wicks soaked in oil. Fines are imposed for deviations from ritual observances. The main pooja (ritual worship) is held in the evening. The Brahmin temple priest carries the Bhagwathi idol on his head and dances around the temple. On the last day of the festival, the idol is taken across fields by the priest and given a ritual bath in a stream. The priests serve a vegetarian feast for the devotees.

Hindu festivals

Besides the folk festivals and ceremonies that are recognised as typically Kodava, quite a few Kodavas have over the years started observing the following Hindu festivals also, in common with their neighbours. Yugadi, the New Year festival as per the lunar calendar, is celebrated in March across Karnataka, and on that day people in Kodagu also eat bevu bella, a mixture of neem leaves and jaggery, and payasa (a sweet dish made with milk and rice).

Shiva Padre or Shiva Rathri is celebrated in late February as the night of Lord Shiva, when devotees refrain from sleep in order to pray, and men in Kodagu wear various disguises and go from house to house during the night. This event is known as kali poraduvo and is meant to entertain the village people as they stay awake that night.

Subrahmanya Sashti is celebrated on a specific day around November or December. On that day, Kodavas observe a fast and gather by a river to enjoy a vegetarian meal cooked by all the villagers together, and visit the Subrahmanya temples.

Mainstream Practises

The following paragraphs compare and contrast the Kodava practices with those that are commonly followed by Hindus.

Among Kodavas, after childbirth, all the members of the okka to which the child belongs are considered to be under ritual pollution, or sutaka, for a week. The ritual pollution of the mother lasts longer, for two months. Among Hindus in general, it is only the mother of the new-born child and the baby who are under ritual pollution for a period that could vary from 3 to 10 days, and the mother is under ritual pollution for varying periods up to nearly 40 days. In some parts of India when a male child is born, a bronze tray is struck to announce his birth. If it is a girl child, a winnowing fan is struck. But among Kodavas, a gun is fired to announce the birth of a boy and a bell-metal plate is struck to announce the birth of a girl. The child is given a name on the twelfth day after childbirth, among both Kodavas and most Hindus.

Like most Hindus, Kodavas usually cremate their dead. Only the corpses of children and pregnant women, and occasionally those of famous persons, are buried. In Kodagu each okka has its own cremation and burial grounds. The fact that, traditionally, the wife of a deceased Kodava man kindles her husband's funeral pyre and vice versa is one of the striking examples of Kodava customs and traditions that differ widely from those of the majority of Hindus. Those who come to pay their respects to the deceased wear white clothes. On the eleventh day after the funeral, those who attended the death ceremony and other relatives attend the maada in honour of the deceased, when they speak of the deceased person and a group of singers sing the polchi paat in praise of him/her. The family of the deceased serve them a grand meal. The okka to which the deceased belonged is considered to be under ritual pollution until the day of the maada.

3. Modern Religion

"Brahminism in Coorg, which found no favour with the Rajahs, appears to be in the ascendency under the liberal patronage of the British Government.11 Rich stipends were drawn from the Government by the Brahminical institutions."

Hindu Monasteries

The Ramakrishna Mission that popularised Vedanta philosophy was based on the teachings of Ramakrishna Paramahansa and his disciple Swami Vivekananda. This Hindu reformist institution revived popularity in Hinduism in lieu of priestly supremacy.

The Ramakrishna Mission and the Vedanta Sangha had a great influence on Kodavas in the early twentieth century. Many Kodavas became followers of these movements, either directly or indirectly. Some of them considered Swami Vivekananda to be their role model and a few even became Hindu monks.

An Ashrama of the Ramakrishna Mission was founded in Ponnampet, South Kodagu and Swami Shambavananda (born Thelapanda Chengappa) became its first head. Likewise Kaveri Ashrama was established in Virajpet town and was headed by Sadguru Appayya Swami (born Palanganda Appayya).

Vegetarianism and Teetotalism

Mainstream Hinduism glorifies notions of vegetarianism and teetotalism, unlike the traditional Kodava folk cult. In contrast to the Vedic ceremonies, Kodavas had meat and liquor during their ceremonies. But as the Kodavas are becoming integrated with the conventional religion, some choose to change their habits accordingly. This process has been gradual and over centuries. Reverence to cattle and not eating beef is what Kodavas have in common with other Hindus.

The temple of Baithurappa, presently the Vayathur Mahadeva temple in Ulikkal, near Vayathur in Kannur district, in Kerala, is one of the important shrines of the Kodavas. The hereditary deva thakka (caretaker of a shrine) of this temple is from the Puggera okka. Tradition holds that the first Puggera deva thakka of Baithurappa temple was a teetotaller and a vegetarian.

In 1883 some prominent Kodavas tried to start a temperance movement, which however failed to make much of an impact. During the 1940s, the Gandhian era, I.M.Muthanna, a writer and educator, was part of a group which advocated teetotalism. He and others in the group went from house to house in Kodagu insisting that people give up alcohol and not even include it in their ceremonies.

Sociologist M.N.Srinivas proposed the term Sanskritisation in his thesis 'Religion and Society among the Coorgs of South India' based on his study of the Kodavas. According to that theory, castes are said to be fluid and are able to rise in the 'hierarchy by adopting vegetarianism and teetotalism'. However, although

Amma Kodavas are vegetarians and teetotallers and are called 'Kaveri brahmins', they are not considered to be higher than Kodavas in the social hierarchy. The few Kodavas who have adopted vegetarianism and teetotalism have not 'risen' to the 'Brahmin' status. M.N.Srinivas's theory is flawed since, according to sociologist Yogendra Singh, it 'neglects non-Sanskrit traditions' such as those of the Kodavas. This is also indicative of the fact that Kodavas traditionally never considered Brahmins to be 'higher' in status than themselves.

In ancient India, animal sacrifice was practised during yajnas and in temples. Human sacrifice was practised in temples, especially in those dedicated to Kali. While human sacrifices have been replaced by animal sacrifices, animal sacrifice to ancestors and spirit-deities is common practice in Kodagu. However, since around April 2016, animal sacrifices, which used to be part of festivals such as the Boad name and the Chaundi theray, are being stopped by the government and other organisations.

Conclusion

Today Kodavas largely identify themselves as Hindus, almost by default, since they do not belong to any of the other major religions in India. While a few have Brahminical poojas, such as gruha pravesha (house-warming ceremony) and Satya Narayana pooja, held in their homes, some have turned vegetarian.

In the present age, Kodavas are sadly losing their unique

identity. This is a loss to pluralism and diversity in India. A people who were kept away from the Vedas, the scriptures of the Hindu religion, by the Brahmins, the priests of the Hindu religion, have come to believe in Brahminism. For ages Kodavas had succeeded in resisting Brahminical supremacy. But presently they seem to be submitting themselves to the Hindu varna (caste) system. They are largely identified as Kshatriyas, the second caste, the martial caste, because Kodava men, free holding farmers and militiamen, carried arms at all times and held government positions under the Rajas in the olden days.

Currently, the State Government has given the Kodavas the Other Backward Caste (Category 3A) reservation status while the Union government has recognised them as a General category with no reservations. The Codava National Council (CNC) organisation has been demanding scheduled tribe status for Kodavas. It has been claiming that the Kodavas as a tribe belonged to no religion. Their website has, under the history section, also identified points by means of which Kodavas are distinguished from 'other Hindus'. The CNC is also demanding that Kodagu be given the status of a Codava Autonomous Region, since Codavas (Kodavas) are a primitive ethnic tribe.

I would like to state that the Kodavas are presently like the mainstream Hindus in some ways and unlike them in other ways. In other words, they definitely follow a distinct way of life which is, however, not completely unrelated to Hinduism. Whether we, Kodavas, call ourselves a sect of Hindus – Kodava Hindus, or followers of an independent Kodava religion is actually a question of perception and therefore of how we label ourselves.

Footnotes :

1. Loosely translated first verse of a Kodava folk song, from the Pattole Palame.
2. Karnataka State Gazetteer: Kodagu district, Kamath, 1993, p.160.
3. Eastern Experiences, Bowring, 1871, p.240.
4. Brahminism refers to the domination of Indian society by the priestly class of Brahmins and their Hindu-ideology.
5. A Social history of India, Dr. S. N. Sadasivan, 2000, p. 316.
6. Coorg Memoirs, Moegling, 1855, p.14.
7. During the Raj, European authorities and missionaries tended to call the 'pagan' (those with religious beliefs different from the mainstream) gods as demons.
8. Imperial Gazetteer of India Mysore and Coorg 1985 [1908], p.297.
9. The complex sacrificial religion that emerged in post-Vedic India (c. 900 BC) under the influence of the dominant priesthood (Brahmans), an early stage in the development of Hinduism. Brahmanism is the central theme and belief of Vedic followers, its thoughts and philosophical concept giving rise to

the primary and socio-religious belief and conduct in Hinduism.

10. Manual of Coorg, Richter, 1870, p. 111-112.
11. Gazetteer of Coorg, Richter, 1870, p.178.

Bibliography

- Bowman, W. D. 1932. The Story of Surnames. London: George Routledge & Sons.
- Bowring, L. 1871. Eastern Experiences. London: H. S. King.
- Bowring, L. 1893 [2009]. Hyder Ali and Tipu Sultan. Delhi: Idarah-I Adabiyat-I Delli.
- Chinnappa, Nadikerianda, 2003 [1924]. Pattole Palame (Translated by Boverianda Nanjamma and Chinnappa into English) Delhi : Rupa.
- Codava National Council, "Codava National Council", Retrieved January 15, 2017, from http://codavanationalcouncil.in
- Engels, F., 1902. The Origin of the Family, Private Property and the State. Chicago: Charles H. Kerr & Co.
- Emeneau, M. B., 'Personal Names of the Coorgs', Journal of the American Oriental Society, Vol. 96, No. 1 (Jan. – Mar., 1976), pp.7-14.
- Kamath, Dr. Suryanath U. 1993. Karnataka State Gazetteer: Kodagu district. Bangalore: Government Press.
- Krishnaiah, D. N. 1974. Kodagina Itihasa. Mysore: Prasanga (Kannada).
- Kutty, K. Govindan. "Tipu Sultan and Doordarshan". Tipu Sultan: Villain or Hero?: An Anthology 56-66 (Sita Ram Goel 1993). New Delhi: Voice of India.

- Moegling, Rev. H. 1855. Coorg Memoirs: An Account of Coorg and of the Coorg Mission, Bangalore: Wesleyan Mission Press.
- Mill, James; Wilson, Horace Hayman (1858). The history of British India, Volume 5. London: Piper, Stephenson, and Spence.
- Richter, Rev. G. 1870. Gazetteer of Coorg, Mangalore: Basel Mission.
- Rice, B. L. 1914. Epigraphia Carnatica, Vol. 1 Madras : Madras Government Publications.
- Sadasivan, Dr. S. N. 2000. A Social history of India. New Delhi: APH Publishing.
- Sri Kaveri Ashrama. 1975. Devara Naamaavali Maththu Stotramaala sangraha. Virajpet: Kodagu Teachers Cooperative Printers.
- Srinivas, M. N. 1952. Religion and Society among the Coorgs of South India. United Kingdom: Oxford University Press.
- Wilks, Mark. 1869 [1811]. Historical Sketches of the South India in an attempt to trace the History of Mysoor. Madras: Higginbotham.
- W.W.Hunter. 1985 [1908] Imperial Gazetteer of India: Mysore and Coorg. New Delhi: Usha.

Roona Uthappa Ballachanda

Roona Uthappa Ballachanda

is a freelance writer and editor who was born and raised in Virajpet, Kodagu. She has an MA in English Literature from the University of Mysore, a Master of Social Work degree from Southern Illinois University at Carbondale, USA and a Writing Certificate from Exeter College, University of Oxford, UK.

THE WAY FORWARD: KODAVAS SHOULD BE GIVEN RELIGIOUS MINORITY STATUS

ROONA UTHAPPA BALLACHANDA

Ever wondered why Kodavas and Kodagu are so much at the mercy of outsiders?

Most activism that we see among Kodavas these days is focused on being defensive, on protecting ourselves from external onslaught, rather than on working together to prevent such blitzing in the first place. People are no strangers to the fact that succumbing to outside pressure, persuasion and plots has been an integral part of Kodava history.

As the native inhabitants of a beautiful land, we have done precious little to save this land from the greedy eyes of those who only wish to milk it for all its worth. Worse still, many Kodavas have also participated in this shameful act, be it as innocent victims, ignorant dupes or wily crooks looking to increase their personal wealth.

Be that as it may, the question remains: how did this happen and why is it still happening? And what does this have to do with religion?

The answer lies in a complex web of nature, nurture,

education, social and political ties, religious beliefs and the psychological characteristics of the Kodava people. Whew! How do we even begin to unravel that one?

Living in geographical isolation for centuries, grappling with the elements of nature, fighting the straightforward battle for survival in dense forests inhabited by wild animals enabled the Kodava to grow strong and self-sufficient.

However, the ability to deal with the machinations of man was not very well developed among Kodavas. This is only natural – after all we learn best to deal with those things that are a normal part of our background.

The Kodava upbringing for centuries was very cloistered, both due to their isolated environment and clan living with close bonds of kinship. In fact, all historical accounts of clan living point towards a sheltered way of life where a few people assumed responsibilities for the welfare of all, and leadership was everything.

If you had a good clan leader, followed the clan rules, and allowed older, more experienced people to be responsible for your well-being, you lived a good life. Maybe this was a way of compensating for the extremely rough natural conditions of the district. What's unfortunate is that this concept became so ingrained in the Kodava psyche that when outsiders came to Kodagu and assumed a leadership position, we let them.

We knew how to wage war against Tipu's overt attacks but were clueless about the far more sophisticated attempts to subdue us that were used by Veeraraja who started the Haleri dynasty in Kodagu. Although in retrospect, the monarchy brought peace and stability for a while by putting an end to the constant infighting of the local Nayakas and helped unite Kodagu against the invasions of Hyder Ali and Tipu Sultan, it still doesn't mitigate the fact that when faced with smart strategizing, Kodavas were helpless.

So, the tale continues. Tipu openly fought with the aim to convert Kodavas to Islam and the warrior Kodavas vehemently opposed it. Christian missionaries preached zealously about the benefits of becoming a Christian believer and the proud Kodava ignored it.

Hinduism, on the other hand, used a subtle, assimilative approach. It gradually incorporated our deities, beliefs, rituals, songs, dances and our rivers, hills, ancestors and spirits into Hindu mythology and philosophy. The naïve Kodava swallowed it hook, line and sinker. We let it fill the gaps in our spiritual needs, made misguided efforts to fit into the Hindu caste system by calling ourselves or allowing us to be called Kshatriyas and subconsciously cultivated a certain degree of detachment towards our original Kodava faith.

The British swept in, camouflaged as saviours. They experimented with coffee growing, destroying priceless forest land in the process, before realizing the wisdom of native methods of plantation, while we watched mutely from the sidelines. The Kodava hunted only during certain seasons and had rules to minimize wildlife damage. Nevertheless, we didn't think it necessary to prevent the kings and British officers from casually emptying our forests of wildlife in their pursuit of grandiose pleasure.

We enriched our language with borrowed words and beggared it by letting go of unique Kodava words rooted in our land, climate and culture. We enthusiastically sought education and accepted it happily when Kannada and English were established as the medium of instruction in our schools, where the Kodava language did not even merit a place as a subject – in much the same way that Hindi was accepted when it was named the official language in the constitution. And, once alien written languages came in, they brought their own influences, further ripping away the 'Kodava-ness' of a Kodava child. This also drastically reduced the possibility of the Kodava language growing and developing, with an erudite literature of its own.

Then came Indian Independence and the birth of democracy in India. After a brief period of respite, when Coorg (Kodagu) was an independent state with home-grown administrators, it went on to become an integral part of Karnataka State.This had its advantages as the people of Kodagu gained access to a wider geographical area for jobs, but it also served to increase the number of people intent on looting the natural wealth of Kodagu. Moreover, another layer of identity cloaked the Kodava – that of a Kannadiga.

So, now, we are Kodavas, Hindus, Kannadigas and Indians. Which identity takes precedence? How should we live? Can we be everything? One thing? Nothing?

This is important, because what we think of ourselves will have a huge influence on how we live our lives, our loyalties and our priorities.

Do I consider myself a Kodava and fight for the survival of Kodagu? Or do I consider myself an Indian and ignore any depredations that take place in Kodagu, because my fellow countrymen and women have a right to go anywhere and do anything they want within the country, as long as it is legal and lawful?

Do I as a Kodava fight for the survival of Devarakadus because they are my sacred groves, my place of worship? Or, do I as a Hindu, turn a blind eye to illegal encroachment or government sanctioned deforestation of these groves, as there are plenty of other temples around, where I can seek proximity to God?

To a certain extent, the very plurality of Indian culture, gives people multiple identities, and life becomes one long balancing act. What helps keep it stable is one's fundamental identity and place in society. Additionally, indigenous cultures are also deeply committed to keeping the natural environment more or less intact. Cultures that developed organically within the surrounding eco-system are invaluable in preserving biodiversity and ecological balance, ultimately playing a significant role in the continuation of humanity on earth.

The combination of large-scale migration and urbanization in India has affected most citizens in one way or the other. Different communities have come up with different ways to deal with this. However the task is less complicated when it involves only symbols, language, rituals and customs.

For a landed community like ours, in a land-starved country like India, the battle for cultural continuity becomes extremely thorny. We are already experiencing this in our fight to protect our Jamma land rights and to prevent the destruction of our forest wealth in the name of development. Nevertheless, we have to find ways to help continue our cultural existence.

There is a huge clamour the world over, to support and protect indigenous peoples, their land, culture and biodiversity. The United Nations has responded by organizing various chapters, forums and committees to research indigenous issues and advise national and state governments on how to protect and help keep alive the varied native cultures of the world. It is up to us to outline those instruments that can help our goals and make use of them to the best of our ability.

If we wish to seek Constitutional assistance, the only viable option is getting the religious minority tag, as there is no such thing as an ethnic or cultural minority according to the Constitution of India. As for getting any kind of autonomy, be it as a state or as an independent region, it appears to be a hopeless cause. Kodavas belong to Kodagu but Kodagu belongs to many different peoples and communities. Moreover, Kodagu is the proverbial golden goose and no political party will be willing to commit political or economic suicide by granting the district any measure of autonomy.

Nevertheless, as the saying goes, a journey of a thousand miles begins with a single step.

Getting independent parliamentary representation and religious minority status for Kodavas as allowed by the Constitution are probably the first steps.

Article 29 in The Constitution of India states,

"Any section of the citizens residing in the territory of India or any part thereof having a distinct language, script or culture of its own shall have the right to conserve the same."

This clause is very broad in its declaration, and gives us leeway to include all our traditional concepts, including customs, rituals, community laws, land tenure systems, traditional methods of village and forest land organization etc., as an indispensable part of our cultural construct.

It can also give us a solid reason to keep our gun rights going. The 'gun' is not merely a weapon for Kodavas, it is an integral part of our culture. It is used to announce births and deaths; it has a role in our festivals, and is worshipped during Kailpodh, our change of season festival; it helps us to protect ourselves in our isolated homesteads, and ultimately, is a very important symbol of our martial history and identity.

Our community today is hugely concerned about conserving Kodava culture, ethnicity and identity, and for very valid reasons. But, culture cannot be 'preserved' like raw mangoes in brine; it is a dynamic organism, gradually morphing into new forms in the process of providing its followers a strong anchor in human society. Yet, there are irrefutable reasons why any given culture should be allowed to keep its distinctiveness intact while it grows and develops.

Culture and tradition, handed down the generations is the essence of one's past – it contains priceless ancestral wisdom and provides a roadmap for a person's journey through life. Our practices of ancestor veneration and nature worship have tremendous metaphorical significance to us as Kodavas. It helps clan members to maintain a strong feeling of kinship as blood relatives and descendants of the same ancestors. It acts as psychological support in times of distress and turmoil. It keeps us grounded in our culture, helps build the foundation of our cultural identity and serves to remind us of our place in history and society.

This is of supreme importance, especially today, because young Kodavas have no way to 'feel Kodava', as the Kodava way of life is fast disappearing. Disturbingly, many seem to think that being Kodava is all about drinking alcohol, eating meat, wearing the traditional costume, dancing to the valaga music and feeling insulted at the slightest provocation on behalf of Kodavame.

Even more disturbing is the fact that concepts of 'racial purity' and 'racial superiority' figure more and more often in the current Kodava discourse. There are no pure races in a country and civilization as old as India and racial superiority is a blatantly dangerous, disgusting and incorrect belief.

History has shown us the painful effects of racial exclusivity notions and we do not want to incite similar activities. But, when a huge void is left behind by the dissolution of the old ways, such things can happen. So, the further away we go from the traditional, clan and nature-based Kodava lifestyle, the more important it becomes for us to ensure that the Kodava beliefs and values are developed, protected and practiced at least at a symbolic level.

Worshipping our rivers and forest deities helps keep in mind their importance in our lives and prompts us to work towards conserving them and their sanctity. It inspires us to protect and preserve our environment. It gives us deep knowledge about the working of the natural world and how best to utilize it for legitimate human need. Whatever other religious practices we may adopt, these two aspects of our culture should never be forgotten. But, is that possible?

To make it possible, we need some emotional distance from all the new religious practices adopted by us in the recent centuries and make a conscious effort to develop Kodava faith and thought.

Getting a religious minority tag would open doors that will be helpful to this cause. Kodava institutions can incorporate research and practices geared towards development and propagation of the Kodava belief system. For instance, many Catholic institutions offer retreats to Catholic students – a time and place to sit back, contemplate and talk about their religious concerns and spiritual dilemmas. At present, we have no avenues for religious or spiritual discussion based on the Kodava faith. We have no place for organized cultural education, dissemination and discussion.

We do have the 'Kodava Samajas' with their associated club houses, but when you walk in there, all you get is the strong stench of stale cigarette smoke and alcohol fumes, with attendant card tables and other such props for enjoyment.

Where are the libraries? Where is the space for Kodava children to learn at the knees of their elders? We no longer live in our ancestral homes in our villages, where culture was absorbed by osmosis and practiced from birth to death. Nuclear families in towns and cities are the norm now. How will younger generations of Kodavas learn anything about Kodava culture or contribute towards its growth, if there is no space for it in their lives? How can Kodava thought and faith develop, how can Kodavame endure into the future if there is no focused effort to create and circulate knowledge through classes, workshops, retreats, books and libraries?

Observing Kodava rituals, performing our dances and celebrating our festivals can only take us so far. In fact, all that we practice today are remnants of our past, with a dwindling number of participants. The chief reason for this is the deep disconnect between the ancient Kodava and the modern Kodava.

Kodavame developed to a certain level and then became stagnant because Kodava people began to disperse in many different directions. And a new type of Kodavas came up – modern, urbanized, liberated and utterly clueless about how to maintain their Kodava self in the face of all the enticing new concepts around them, leading to the gradual loss of their traditional lifestyle. Additionally, education brought with it an inquiring mind, a questioning attitude and skepticism towards the esoteric and mystical, towards anything that is not based on empirical evidence.

As more and more Kodavas join the educated crowd, increasingly disregarding long-held religious beliefs, the more urgent it becomes for us to have public debates and discussions in an encouraging atmosphere. Cultural confusion may seem harmless at the moment, but in the long run it can have serious repercussions on both the individual and society. If we don't have a strong sense of self, if we don't take the time to spell out what makes us who we are and what is important to our identity, we won't be able to protect ourselves against external influence and aggression. And if the Kodava is destroyed, Kodagu will follow soon enough.

The religious minority tag will give us a strong leg to stand on, both in legal battles as well as in community endeavors. To get the religious minority tag, the Kodava belief system must be recognized as a religion first, and Kodava people should be willing to give up their accepted non-Kodava faith, if they have one. In other words, we need to unlearn what we have learned over the past few centuries. Is this feasible? Anyway, for all its flaws, the beauty of democracy is that people have complete freedom to follow the faith of their choice. So, establishing a Kodava religion and deeming it a minority one, need not necessarily prevent people from continuing to believe in what they believe at a personal level, in addition to their original faith.

Getting a separate identity as a distinct religion will have a psychological effect on the community. It will create a deeper consciousness in the minds of the Kodava people regarding their heritage and this will go a long way towards protecting cultural continuity, which is of utmost importance to the continued existence of humanity on earth. Also, as a religious minority group whose identity is based on land ownership, we can ask for laws to safeguard our sacred groves and our traditional land tenure systems. We will be in a stronger position to fight against laws that seek to dispossess us of our revered lands, or stop our traditional methods of worship, etc.

How do we go about doing this? There is no provision in the Indian legislature or judiciary to create or recognize a religion. So far, history has taken care of that. So, the Kodava bid to be recognized as a separate religion must start with work from within. The community should come together to establish the Kodava way of life as a distinct religion on its own, based on nature and ancestor worship, our sacred groves and forest shrines which are our temples, and get it recognized by the legal and political system of the country.

Recently, the Jains succeeded in getting a religious minority status by proving that despite similarities with Hinduism, they are a separate religion. Our approach should also be along similar lines, as the Kodava belief system too has similarities with Hinduism but it has a different origin as well as rituals and practices contrary to established Hindu customs.

The constitution declares that we have a right to conserve our culture. Research and scholarship shows that continuation of diverse cultures is very important for the continuation of humanity. Experience has revealed that the fragmentation of the Kodava way of life has had a huge negative impact on the environment with far reaching consequences.

A lot of cohesive energy is being spent on passionate pleas to save Kodagu and the Kodavas, but what we also need is a pragmatic analysis of reality and focused action that takes recourse to the expertise of scholars and the laws of the nation. We should also keep in mind that the Kodava case is unique and we cannot afford to look for solutions in established practices alone. We should carve a legal or constitutional path that can tackle the varied needs of a cultural minority like ours and maybe set a precedent for other such communities to follow. And, in the process, for once in our collective history, be an agent of change rather than merely a victim of it. With the blessings of our ancestors, let us invoke our warrior days of old to fight this battle for survival... and come out victorious!

EPILOGUE: ARE KODAVAS (COORGS) HINDUS?

P.T. BOPANNA

Are Kodavas (Coorgs) Hindus? The answer is both 'yes' and 'no'! If one defines Hinduism as a way of life, then Kodavas are Hindus. If one looks at Hinduism from the rigid caste-centric angle, then Kodavas are not Hindus.

Dr. Sarvepalli Radhakrishnan (1888-1975), former President of India, who was one of the most erudite Hindu scholars of all times, has said: "Hinduism is not a religion, but a commonwealth of religions. It is more a way of life than a form of thought. The theist and the atheist, the skeptic and the agnostic may all be Hindus if they accept the Hindu system of culture and life. Hinduism insists not on religious conformity but on a spiritual and ethical outlook of life. Hinduism is not a sect but a fellowship of all who accept the law of right and earnestly seek for the truth."

The concept of Hinduism as propounded by Dr. Radhakrishnan was lofty and incorporated the essence of the ancient Indian civilization. But in the present era of 'Mandal' and 'Kamandal' politics, it is caste which determines the Hindu identity.

Kodavas are a unique community who live in Kodagu (Coorg, as the British called it), the smallest district in Karnataka. Very little is known about the origin of this community of warriors who have lived on the slopes of the Western Ghats of South India from time immemorial. This land-owning community known for its martial traditions, has a distinct culture that is strikingly different from that of the neighbouring cultures.

If caste is used as the yardstick to ascertain whether Kodavas are Hindus, then this small community numbering less than two lakh, are certainly not Hindus because they do not belong to any Hindu caste and there is no caste system among the Kodavas.

Another important factor which characterizes the Hindu caste system is the belief in the supremacy of Brahmins. Judged from this yardstick too, Kodavas are not Hindus because there is hardly any role for Brahmins in the various Kodava ceremonies related to birth, marriage and death. It is the elders in the community who conduct all rituals.

Kodavas are basically ancestor and nature worshippers. Every Kodava is a member of a patrilineal okka (clan) that has descended from a common ancestor. The Karanava, the first ancestor of the clan, is revered as a God, and Kodavas worship the ancestral spirit, their Guru karona. While their ancestors are their guiding spirits, Kodavas consider their elders as their living guides. The youngsters greet their elders by touching their feet three times and the latter invoke their ancestors when they bless them.

Every ancestral home (ainmane) invariably has a kaimada, a small shrine nearby, where prayers to ancestors are offered. The ancestral homes face the East, and Kodavas start their daily chores by opening the main door of the house and saluting the sun in prayer. And idol worship is non-existent. A lamp (bolcha) or hanging lamp (thook bolcha) is lit, both at dawn and dusk, to invoke the blessings of the ancestors. The lamp is kept in the nellakki nadu bade (central hall in the ancestral home). The sacred area around the lamp is empty and no idol or photograph adorns the space. The same goes for the space where meedi (offerings to the ancestors) is kept. Most of the important decisions are solemnised in front of the lamp. However, in recent years in some ainmanes, framed photos of Hindu gods are kept in these sacred spaces. There are no idols in the kaimada, the central place of ancestor worship, where the annual ritual of Karonang kodpo is held in memory of the ancestors. A few kaimadas have figurines resembling humans, to represent their ancestors.

To sum up, Kodavas believe that there is a direct link between the living and their ancestors.

Kodavas worship river Kaveri as water and not as an image. During Kaveri Sankramana to celebrate the birth of the river, goddess Kaveri is symbolically represented by a decorated coconut or cucumber.

Another major deviation from mainstream Hinduism is the practice of meedi offerings for ancestors which consist of food items, including non-vegetarian dishes like pork, the signature dish of the Kodavas. Along with the food, liquor is also offered to invoke the blessings of ancestors. This practice is inconsistent with the rigid notions of 'pollution' practiced by orthodox Hindus.

Though Kodavas had maintained their own religious identity of ancestor and nature worship, things began to change after 1600 AD with the advent of the Lingayat or Haleri kings in Kodagu. The Haleri Rajas built Hindu temples and appointed deva thakkas (temple headmen) to propagate their faith among the Kodavas. Tulu and Kannada-speaking Brahmin priests were brought from outside Kodagu to perform pooja at these temples.

Over the years, temples dedicated to deities such as Bhagavati or Muthappan have come up in Kodagu. These deities were mainly imported from Kerala. Igguthappa, the god dedicated to rain and harvest, was also one such import from Kerala.

Kodavas also worship a few spirit deities like Kulika, Pashanamurthi, etc. who were imported from Tulunad or Kerala.

In today's circumstances, it is essential to maintain Kodava identity, instead of trying to embrace mainstream Hinduism. The belief in ancestor and nature worship is much more rational and scientific, compared to belief in myths and rituals which are alien to Kodava religious practices.